Writing Personal Poetry

PRAISE FOR SHEILA BENDER

Writing Personal Poetry

"Reading Bender's book is like joining a poetry workshop where you not only have a terrific teacher, you meet wonderful new friends."
—Jim Bertolino, author of
What Water Says and *Snail River*

Writing Personal Essays

Bender's creative, yet practical methods would serve potential E.B. Whites equally well in the classroom, with a writing group, or at the kitchen table.
—Patricia Hassler, *Booklist*

Writing in a Convertible With the Top Down

I used to think there could never be a book about writing as good as Natalie Goldberg's *Writing Down the Bones*. But *Writing in a Convertible* really is, as its subtitle says, A Unique Guide for Writers.
—Patricia Holt, *San Francisco Chronicle*

Wise and constructive. These letters shed light on writing as a process and let you feel you're sitting in on an intimate, empowering writer's group.
—Judith Applebaum, author of
How to Get Happily Published

Love From the Coastal Route

The clarity—both emotional and linguistic—of these poems is testament to the work Sheila Bender has set herself: to understand as far as she can and then to admit, in the presence of mystery, that ignorance which forms for us, every day, three square meals. I love these poems for that diligence and for themselves. —William Matthews author of
Blues If You Want, Time & Money and *Sleek for the Long Flight*

Near the Light

When I get tired of the press of houses and faces and clocks, I go to the ocean, listen to the advice of the surf and the tide. Sheila Bender's poems are like this. They are windows of light that we are welcomed to look through, and looking out, we find ourselves comforted.
—James Masao Mitsui, author of
From a Three-Cornered World and *After the Long Train Poems*

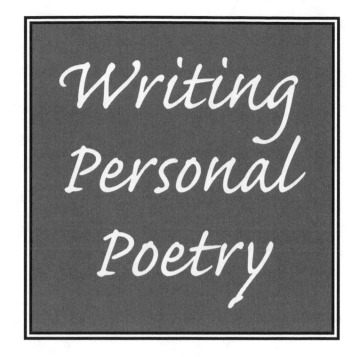

Writing Personal Poetry

CREATING POEMS

FROM YOUR

LIFE EXPERIENCES

SHEILA BENDER

WRITER'S DIGEST BOOKS
CINCINNATI, OHIO

Visit our Web site at www.writersdigest.com for information on more resources for writers.

To receive a free biweekly E-mail newsletter delivering tips and updates about writing and about Writer's Digest products, send an E-mail with "Subscribe Newsletter" in the body of the message to newsletter-request@writers digest.com or register directly at our Web site at www.writersdigest.com.

02 01 00 99 98   5 4 3 2 1

Library of Congress Cataloging-in-Publication Data

Bender, Sheila
    Writing personal poetry / by Sheila Bender.—1st ed.
        p.   cm.
    Includes bibliographical references and index.
    ISBN 0-89879-813-2 (hardcover : alk. paper)
    1. Poetry—Authorship. 2. Self in literature. 3. Persona (Literature) I. Title.
PN1059.A9B46   1998
808.1—dc21   98-39747
                                                                 CIP

Edited by Jack Heffron and Chantelle Bentley
Production edited by Jeff Crump
Cover design by Clare Finney
Cover photography by Bill Westheimer

The permissions on page ix constitute an extension of this copyright page.

ABOUT THE AUTHOR

Sheila Bender holds a masters of arts in creative writing from the University of Washington. She teaches in the Northwest at Puget Sound-area workshops, colleges and universities as well as in Tucson, Arizona, for continuing education programs. A new collection of her poems entitled *Sustenance* is available from Daniel and Daniel Publishing, P.O. Box 1525, Santa Barbara, CA 93102. Her other books include *Writing in a New Convertible With the Top Down*, coauthored with Christi Killien (Blue Heron Publishing, 1997), *The Writer's Journal: 40 Contemporary Writers and Their Journals* (Dell Publishing, 1997); and *Writing Personal Essays: How to Shape Your Life Experiences for the Page* (Writer's Digest Books, 1995).

ACKNOWLEDGMENTS

I wish to thank Jack Heffron, my editor at Writer's Digest Books, for his thoughtful help in shaping this manuscript. I want to thank my agent, Elizabeth Wales of the Wales Literary Agency, Inc., for fostering opportunities for me to write instructional books. And I wish to thank each of the new and experienced poets whose starts, revisions and realized poems are included in this book. Their work will help my readers learn to begin, shape and finish poems of their own. And, as always, I wish to thank Kurt VanderSluis, my husband, for his computer help, which pulled this manuscript out of the ethers over and over.

For Poetry, which brought my life to me,
and for all my students and loved ones
who made that life the one I want to live.

Should we say the self, once perceived, becomes the soul?
—*Theodore Roethke*

PREFACE

During the year that I worked on this book, I lived in Birmingham, Michigan; Tucson, Arizona; and Port Townsend and Seattle, Washington. I met for sessions with one group of students in my Seattle dining room, with another group in a Tucson desert townhouse, with some around their kitchen tables over cups of tea and with others through faxes, E-mail and regular mail. I worked with people aged eighteen to ninety. They wanted to begin or continue writing poetry. I shared the exercise chapters of this manuscript with them; then, from the writings they created and my responses and coaching, I shaped the later, instructional chapters. I am proud of their work, but most importantly, I am awed by their ability to use the exercises to mine the depths of their experience and perception. I have included author names (and, in the back of the book, biographical notes) on most all of the poem starts and revisions. However, occasionally, I have left a name off a poem for one of two reasons: Either I used an early draft without showing any finished revision and didn't want to embarrass a beginner, or a beginner wrote a beautiful poem but felt reluctant to be identified because of the poem's content. In both cases, I have willingly respected the authors' privacy and am grateful that the authors allowed me to use their material for instructional purposes.

W.H. Auden said that "there is only one thing that all poetry must do; it must praise all it can for being as for happening." But to be poetry there must be a kind of harmony, which according to Paul Valéry, "ought not to be definable; when it can be defined it is imitative harmony and that is not good." There is, he went on to say, "The impossibility of defining the relation, together with the impossibility of denying it. . . ."

Poets learn to recognize these two basic qualities in their work fastest by sharing their works in progress with other poets. In a writing workshop, peers bring in their work in progress and collect responses from sensitive, trusted listeners who enjoy seeing work develop. When an experienced poet facilitates this kind of workshop, new poets benefit from her knowledge, focus and dexterity with the craft. I hope that readers of my book feel as if many poets are in one living room, sharing their new writing with the interested group and searching with me for ways to sculpt poems from these beginnings.

Poetry Is Always
a Good Idea

This past March I met with a friend whom I have been sharing poems in progress with since the seventies, when we found each other in a poetry workshop at the University of Washington. Outside of class we became each other's audience for new and developing poems. Graduate school is behind us, but we continue to get together and discuss our work. We give each other books of poetry we have heard about or enjoyed ourselves. For my birthday, my friend gave me a book of essays about poetry. I was slow to start reading it. Perhaps I was reluctant to be reading about poetry rather than writing it. Or maybe I was worried that I would learn from the book's author, Pulitzer Prize and National Book Critics Circle Award winner Louise Glück, that "I was doing it wrong."

But when I began to read I was drawn into the book. In *Proofs and Theories, Essays on Poetry*, Glück says writing a poem begins with a haunting, as if the finished poem already exists somewhere. In that way, she says, the poem is like a lighthouse, "except that, as one swims toward it, it backs away." "Yes," I heard myself say. "I have felt that!"

The poet must then delve into a period of concentrated work. Glück says this "engagement is absorbing as nothing else I have ever in my life known." But when the poem is finished and "becomes what it was first perceived to be, a thing always in existence," the poet "isn't a poet anymore," but "simply someone who wishes to be one." Yes, I have felt that too!

Underneath the busy hours of raising a family, having a job, participating on committees, buying cars, paying bills, grading papers, writing reports, and finding out why your phone is full of static and your modem keeps losing its signal, you are probably looking for a quiet, contemplative time to find that lighthouse-that-already-is and for help learning to recognize it and bring it to the page. You may also be afraid that finding it might change your life.

Don't let the idea of new perception frighten you. I have learned to take myself away from the telephone, go for a walk or a bicycle ride or pretend for a few hours that I am traveling in a new country and doing what I would do there—I take in the sights, sounds, smells, tastes and "feels" of life. (Of course, actually debarking to a faraway location works, though it just can't be done as easily or often.) When I have cleared some space inside myself, the words begin to come and they fill the air around me like positive ions after a thunderstorm. It feels good to be in this air. Composing, I feel as if I am handed from word to word, until they set me down, my feet on the ground—on the ground, that is, of some passage or new understanding or deeply felt experience. I consider this a wonderful benefit of being a poet, even if knowing what is at the bottom of my mind and in the very inside of my heart requires that I make changes: to live my life as my life asks me to live it.

I look at it this way: Poetry, like dreams, will eventually break through into every person's consciousness, even the tightest icono-clast's. It has to, because poetry (which can be defined as meaning felt and understood in the flow of sound) is life itself, and life is stronger than anyone's psychological dam. Luckily, poetry has the ability to allow the flow of life through in manageable amounts. The life-energy that poetry taps nurtures elasticity in our beings, so we can handle more of life's complexity, and accept how a thing and its opposite coexist. This coming to terms can be accomplished by writing poems from our experiences, whether they are learning com-puter programs, cooking dinner, commuting or dealing with aging.

As I write now, I am remembering an afternoon in 1991, shortly after a book of my poems, *Love From the Coastal Route*, was published. I ran into an acquaintance in a bookstore. She had just found my book on the shelf. After some conversation, I said I had to get home and do my laundry. My acquaintance stood there trying to put these two parts of me together. We had a good laugh at the thought that poets do laundry.

Poets are very much of this world, using images of dinners with burnt vegetables, children wearing shorts in summer and driveways leading to suburban homes. We cook, clean and take out the garbage. The images from what we experience enter our poems and sometimes even help us build metaphors for thinking about poetry. This happened to me during the early stages of my work on this book, when I saw the movie *Sabrina*.

Sabrina thinks she has persuaded a business tycoon she's known since childhood, and with whom she has fallen in love, to go with her to Paris. She believes that in Paris he will develop vulnerability and find happiness in love. But he goes back on his promise, telling her he has only feigned interest in Paris and in her. Shocked and saddened, Sabrina reaches for one of the plane tickets resolutely announcing, "Paris is always a good idea."

After the movie, I kept hearing, "*Poetry* is always a good idea." Writing poetry is how I came of age (though I didn't start until I was thirty-two). I achieved grace and fluidity in my inner life and authenticity where before I'd faked parts of who I was.

The tycoon realizes he loves Sabrina and follows her to Paris. He is in time to embrace her at the front door of their new life.

When you choose to write poetry (and rechoose every time you start a new poem), you may experience the same struggle the film's male lead did in choosing Paris over his role as maker of big business deals. You may realize you have denied yourself what you desire (to write poetry), just as the business tycoon denied the love he wanted, because it seems out of character. Like him, you may have denied inner questions and experiences in order to be rewarded in the outer world, or to keep the peace or avoid pain. You may have felt your ability with language too weak to write poems, just as the tycoon felt underdeveloped in his ability to love. You may have lacked a person in your life who, like Sabrina, says "You can do this."

My book is designed to help you with a lifelong commitment to poetry, whether you desire to write first poems, better poems or more poems. Working with the discussions, exercises and examples will help you build confidence as a poet and as a person who uses words to experience truth, who remains vulnerable to experience, and who has come to know the various feeling tones of the world.

Set your pen to paper and live for poetry! Dwell in its wondrous city, whole and full-hearted.

CHAPTER ONE

Personal Poetry and Why We Write It

An act of imagination is an act of self-acceptance.
　　—*Richard Hugo*
　　Triggering Towns: Lectures and Essays on Poetry and Writing

V: It's a very difficult life, being a poet. Like going to bed on TV, with everybody looking. Like keeping a diary for the world's eyes. You have to be open for inspection, reveal all the dirty and beautiful things that happen to you. If you hide something, it will kill your poems. Sometimes I think it's too terrible . . . like being in a zoo. K: But at least, Andrei, we're our own keepers.
　　—*Andrei Voznesensky and Stanley Kunitz*
　　"Blood and Poetry Are the Same:
　　A Conversation With Andrei Voznesensky"

Personal poems are born of the examination of the elements of your life. Writing poetry, you search for the form of emotions in the sounds of words, in their denotations and connotations. Your search ends in insight earned from the music your poem makes and the images it puts together.

Personal poems are not merely words that paint a picture of your life (which is what one does in descriptive prose). They are not accounts of being wronged (that's for cathartic journal writing). They are not answers to whomever bullied or confused you when you couldn't answer back (letters to the editor, memos and op-ed pieces are what's needed here). Personal poems recount lived experience so it is refelt, but with resolution, rising above the tragic. Poet and critic Ralph Mills Jr. wrote:

... the poet invites us to share in his pursuit of identity; to witness the dramatization of the daily events of his experience—so closely resembling our own; to be haunted by the imagery of his dreams or the flowing stream of his consciousness; to eavesdrop on relationships with friends and lovers; to absorb the shock of his deep-seated fears.

Each poet, he says, wants "to speak to us, without impediment, from the deep center of a personal engagement with existence." Frank Bidart says that writing poetry is "articulating the things that are most central" to us, that we "attempt to tell the truth, to be honest even at personal cost."

Contemporary poets strip away devices that distance readers from their poems. They speak so their words will be understood and felt. To close the distance between themselves and their experience, and between themselves and their readers, they use the word "I." They use the details of their daily lives and usually stay away from forced rhyme schemes that sound formal and manufactured.

THE NATURE OF GOOD POETRY

If you have never written for publication or read your work to an audience, you might assume you would write personal poetry just for yourself, for the cathartic value. Why, then, would you be concerned with the reader? The answer lies in the nature of good poetry.

A good personal poem is not one that rests with pat ideas of what life is supposed to feel like. It captures a particular life and time. It captures the poet in the process of struggling to find out what this inner experience is. If the struggle is genuinely felt, resolution will be discovered as a result of writing the poem. Then the poem will move those who read it. Robert Frost is often quoted as having said if there is no discovery for the writer, there will be no discovery for the reader. I think the reverse is worth remembering, too. If the reader can find no discovery, the writer has not fully written the poem. In considering a poem for a reader, the poet must stretch, and in doing so the poet makes further contact with the self.

This idea is born of my experience writing poetry and teaching others to write it. But I find myself wanting to share what other poets have said as well. There is a long tradition among poets of quoting those who have influenced their thinking, and it is in this tradition that I quote numerous poets in my discussions. Not only will you encounter various wordings for notions that are difficult to articulate, you will also learn the names of poets who have written on poetry so you can read further yourself.

Stephen Dunn writes in "The Good, the Not So Good," an essay on poetry in his book *walking light*:

> The not so good personal poem makes us feel uncomfortable the way the problems of strangers do. We're not quite sure why they're telling us what they're telling us. At best, the problem is interesting, but we feel more like voyeurs than listeners who have some stake in what we're being told.

The antidote to creating this sort of poem is to be aware that you are striving for a poem in which readers (including yourself) *experience* the struggle, not merely the reportage. Lawrence Raab reminds poets in his article "Choosing the Wrong Subject" (*Associated Writing Programs Chronicle*, December 1997) that we only think we know what a poem is about when we start it. As the poet engages with creating the poem, the subject of the poem expands or contracts and changes. Raab says, "To learn to write a poem is to learn how to have those ideas necessary for that particular poem. In this sense, the making of each poem is, for the poet, an education." Often, it is the response of readers that shows an author if the struggle for that education is actually in the poem, or if what is written is merely a recording of "the problems of a stranger."

WHAT IS THIS FEELING?

In writing personal poetry, we must ask ourselves questions: What is this feeling? Where did it come from? We search for the answer, not through logic, but through the words, sounds and rhythms that arise when we engage language in making tangible our sensory and emotional experience. The result is that the answer is embodied in the search itself. That is why Raab says to learn to write a poem is to learn to have those ideas necessary for the poem. The answer, the truth the poet finds, is integrally bound to the search the poet is making, and, therefore, it cannot be uttered apart from the images and sounds with which it arrives. We listen to the syntax and tone of what we are writing to find out what we are writing about. The words, sounds and rhythms that sound right are right. However, you would not have known what was right unless you wrote the poem.

William Stafford summed it up:

> A writer is not so much someone who has something to say as he is someone who has found a process that will bring about new things he would not have thought of if he had not started to say them.

I would add that a writer is also someone who has learned how to listen to reader response to a work in progress in a way that furthers this process.

WHY WE WRITE POETRY

I have written personal poems by saying something about how sad I felt seeing the wet outline of my husband's swimming trunks through his slacks as we drove after arguing. I have started by describing a traditional tea ceremony I attended with my daughter, and I have started by describing an afternoon drive along the Columbia River with my young son. I've written because I wanted to say how a blue moon in August made me aware of the distance between my traveling daughter and myself.

I didn't know why I was writing any of these poems. I only knew by how I felt that poem-making time had come, that I could start the process that would help me find things to say that I could only find by starting to say them. The outline of the trunks made me so sad. The tea ceremony and the images of the ride with my son were always in my mind's eye. The moon as it looked through binoculars wouldn't leave me alone. My writers groups helped me find, through the members' feelings and curiosities, ways to write the poems I was writing. I got that education and found out the something more I needed to know.

In writing, reading and loving poems, you must become a sensitive audience for your unique and individual voice as well as others. Right now you may feel that you are a better listener than a writer. Or you may feel that you do not yet know how to read and listen to poetry as well as you'd like. Even if you have published poems, you may still find listening to and writing personal poetry daunting. You may experience starting each new poem as if you were hiking a mountain trail, out of shape and lacking guides and equipment.

Later I'll focus on building the skills that will help you with writing
as well as reading and responding to drafts. But first, I want to show
you how I employ the specific in my struggle to answer questions I
pose.

While writing this chapter, I was contemplating how to talk about
the reasons for writing personal poetry, but found I couldn't think
well about the question without involving the landscape (particulars
to which the senses relate) where I was doing the thinking.

I was in Birmingham, Michigan, with my husband, who had a
three-month contract to install a computer network management
system for a large company. Sitting at my computer listening to the
air conditioner, I knew that if I was to think about poetry and why
we write it, I would have to see, feel, taste, touch and smell what
was around me. I had to walk and sweat and let the stickiness accu-
mulate on my skin. I walked in hot and humid Birmingham, searching for a way to say why we write poetry.

I passed through downtown into the adjoining residential neighborhood. New modern residences were sprinkled among colonial
and Cape Cod houses. The modern houses looked sleek and long
like horsetail plants, asparagus or palm trees. The smaller homes
looked intricate as many branched and lobe-leafed oak and maple
trees. It was the poet in me supplying these metaphors.

Side by side with the associations I entertained as I walked, I had
questions: What did the owners of the detailed colonials and Cape
Cods think about the large, plain facades they neighbored? What
did I think? Was it OK for me to compare the new architecture to
prehistoric plants and the older architecture to more recent plants?
What was brewing in the images I was seeing and my own responses
to them that I could use in discussing why we write personal poetry?
Words came to me.

We do not write personal poetry to outdo the Joneses, to stay the
way we are, to live like everybody else or even to judge the correct-
ness of people and events. We write because something inside says
we must and we can no longer ignore that voice. We decide we are
ready to listen to that voice to keep from being ill, to stay sane, to
let our minds flourish in waking as they do in our dreams, to feel
our longing and to do something like meditate or pray.

Although there are generously endowed poetry contests, foundation grants for poets; guest residencies at writers' colonies, colleges
and universities; and publishers who publish beautiful editions of

poetry, we don't write poetry for money. We write it to hear our own voices whisper, sing and yell. We write it to find our connections to life. We write it to create an oasis, a temple, a retreat in a world that rushes relentlessly on, leaving us feeling as if there is little time. Writing poetry helps us find what we must to celebrate life, and it allows us to experience depth.

Writing poetry isn't about contributing to the gross national product or financially supporting a family. We may be able to get on with our lives better for having written a poem, but we write it only because we feel we must.

We write poetry for the same reasons our eyes watch finches eat seed from a sunflower or our ears listen to the lacy hem of a lake's edge sweeping across a pebbled shore. We write for the same reasons we watch automobiles on rainy days move into traffic like ants on spilled lemonade. We are lulled by the world and joined to it by our very cells. We search for those junctures we know are there. Writing poems is a way to search for and experience the joining.

Some people choose other ways to do this. An athlete uses his muscles. An inventor designs mechanisms. An animal lover keeps pets or has a whole farm or animal hospital. A chef uses flour, vegetables and fruit.

A poet takes the time to write because in doing so, he knows once again as I did on my walk, the invigorating conflict of opposites we call life, the pleasant startle into a refreshed way of sensing the world, the strength of community when one is heard and hears.

Writing about my walk was a way to get myself thinking so I could find an answer to the question, "Why do we write poetry?" It occurs to me that we must sometimes ask why we are *not* writing poetry. Poems ask us to speak in our own voices, apart from anyone else in the universe. Despite all of our society's emphasis on individualism, each of us has a mind that works hard to keep our perceptions from changing, that wants to help us fit in.

Experiencing what is in your heart and mind may require that you make changes to live your life—in the form of poetry—as it is asking you to live. Instead of being afraid of what your poetry will tell you, keep in mind that poetry creates and supports elasticity so you can handle more life, more complexity, and more of how one thing and its opposite can be true. The calling to write poetry requires that you brave hearing what is at the bottom of your mind, that you let your psyche bubble up and take shape. This bravery and the subsequent poems may change your life. It may change the lives of those around you. Richard Eberhart said, "If a poet writes to save his soul, he may save the souls of others."

◆ ◆ ◆

A NOTE ABOUT FREE VERSE

My exercises and discussions of writing personal poetry center on using free verse, although some of the examples of poems I use for discussion do observe formal structure. What is free verse? Why do we use it? How is it connected to soul work? What does it mean to choose free verse over formal poetic structures? To answer these questions, I have gone again to the writings of experts.

In the 1940s, Babette Deutsch wrote *Poetry Handbook: A Dictionary of Terms*, which was reprinted for decades. She says that free verse does not obey the rules of fixed meter but relies on cadences which are phrases that fall into symmetrical or nearly symmetrical patterns when speech rhythm is highly organized. English poets such as Milton, Blake and Arnold wrote some poems in free verse before it was named as such, but Walt Whitman is attributed as having influenced American poets toward free verse in his poem "Leaves of Grass" which broke with the tradition of end rhymes.

John Ciardi says in *Dialogue With an Audience*, "Nothing is more powerfully of man [and of woman, of course] than the fact that he [or she] gives off forms. . . . Knowing the form is knowing the person." When we write in free verse, we write in the sound of our unique voice and hear what it says often for the first time.

William Packard, founder of *The New York Quarterly*, writes in his book, *The Poet's Dictionary: A Handbook of Prosody and Poetic Devices*, that in free verse, "the poet must concern him- or herself even more attentively with the organic requirements that grow out of the materials at hand." He explains that "the poet must now at all points stay attuned to the peculiar form and shape of his or her own placements, stanza breaks, and all the other external manifestations of form that previously had been given to poets." It is as if the poet "in a purely intuitive state, may not necessarily be aware of external requirements of form but can trust to creating his or her own order simply by following the impulse of his or her own genius in action."

According to W.H. Auden's 1956 inaugural address at Oxford, "Even when [the poem] employs the diction and rhythms of conversation, it employs them as a deliberate informality, presupposing the norm with which they are intended to contrast." In free verse, the poem must do from inside itself what in formal verse would have been imposed by outer patterns. It must be a rite, as Auden calls a poem: "The form of a rite must be beautiful, exhibiting, for example, balance, closure and aptness to that which it is the form of."

Free verse is the poetic organization that lends itself to capturing the forms Ciardi says we give off. It is in striving to find the free verse of our individual voices that we perceive ourselves and save (or create) the souls of which Eberhart speaks. Free verse lends itself to making important discoveries.

Writing free verse is a tall order, even with its informal and conversational diction. We can learn by understanding and practicing the two stages of writing it: 1) finding our material and 2) shaping our work through listening to the cadences and soul-organized phrasing of our best language. After we talk about allowing ourselves the power to write poetry and ways to read poetry, we will begin practicing the first stage of writing free verse.

CHAPTER TWO

Empowering Yourself to Write Poetry

> *. . . if you do not express your own original ideas, if you do not listen to your own being, you will have betrayed yourself. Also you will have betrayed our community in failing to make your contribution to the whole.*
>
> —Rollo May
> The Courage to Create

In 1976, several years before I discovered Rollo May's wonderful book, I was a mother at home with my then three and one year olds. I wrote poems during their nap times. They weren't good poems; I knew that. They were truncated and lacking in details and music. But I did know that I was more engaged in attempting to write these poems than I had been in anything outside of child care for a long time. What then was keeping me from writing the poems more fully, deeply and completely?

The answer was threefold: inexperience with the craft, a lack of reading contemporary poems and a voice rusty from disuse. I took care of the inexperience by enrolling in poetry writing workshops through the "Free University" and community centers, and later the University of Washington's creative writing program. I learned the names of contemporary poets and the titles of their books. I actually had some of these poets as teachers. I addressed my lack of knowledge of contemporary poetry when I began to read my teachers' poems and poems by people they recommended. I began to subscribe to small press literary magazines and read even more of them in bookstores, newsstands and in the homes of my new "poetry" friends. I learned about listings for poetry readings at universities, colleges, community centers and bookstores. I attended them as regularly as I could. Immersing myself into the world of contemporary American poetry, especially into the poetry of my own Northwest region, helped me learn the craft and practice of poetry. But David Wagoner, my first teacher at the University of Washington, reviewed my beginning efforts this way: He told me I was reducing my voice to a laconic whisper, that I needed to learn to sing loudly and at greater length.

This was the third obstacle, "the voice rusty from disuse." What would it take to sing loudly and at greater length? I asked myself. My new belief that my poetry was not only important to my life, but absolutely crucial to it had helped me begin but even believing this, something else was keeping my voice rusty and unused. What was it? Twenty-eight years! Years of dealing with the cold-war-era thinking that had pervaded my early education. Even going to college and studying psychology in the antiauthoritarian sixties had not eradicated what I had been taught as a child: Art was superfluous because physical strength and scientific and engineering knowledge were crucially needed. I had spent twenty-eight years ignoring my need to study writing and pursuing occupations that would meet with the approval of others. Most disastrous of all, I heard the words of my family training years whenever I felt strongly about something: "You are wrong to feel that way. You have no right to feel that way." Searching to discover what I actually felt and endeavoring to sing it out in poetry did not feel rewarding; it felt more like a breach of the family confidence. When I let myself hope to publish my poems, I felt like a turncoat. The poems I was attempting to write dealt with undoing the effect the dictates of my family had on me so I could learn my own self-identity. And any reader would know how and what I felt! The poems detailed unflattering scenes concerning my mother, my father, my sister and my upwardly mobile marriage, which I was unsure of but the family sanctioned.

Furthermore, these poems seemed one-sided, all about an "unhappy childhood," which William Matthews taught is not the whole truth. "We all have two childhoods, the unhappy one and the happy one," he said. Where was my sense of fairness? Why couldn't I write the happy poems?

How did I manage to write fully then, and keep myself and my poems from dying off as laconic whispers in a pool of guilt? Today, how I did it seems more like a miracle than an act of will, but those who knew me say I was determined. In this chapter, we'll discuss overcoming the emotional obstacles to letting your poetry voice sing. You must write the poems that offer themselves to be written—all of them and when they come. You will be surprised at the turns of events that take place, at the turns of your attention and how you can write from both your childhoods, from all periods of your life, including your ever-evolving present.

ACKNOWLEDGE AND CELEBRATE
YOUR POETIC INTELLIGENCE

In 1983, Harvard educator Howard Gardner published his book *Frames of Mind: The Theory of Multiple Intelligences*, a groundbreaking work that argues for the recognition of human competencies that are separate intelligences in addition to the mathematical and verbal ones currently accepted and measured by IQ tests. The first intelligence Gardner discusses is the linguistic intelligence. This is the competency of the poet. Gardner trusts that a poet will best describe this intelligence, and he quotes Stephen Spender:

> Memory exercised in a particular way is the natural gift of poetic genius. The poet above all else, is a person who never forgets certain sense impressions which he has experienced and which he can relive again and again as though with all their original freshness.

Gardner writes that the poet possesses a high degree of competency with the core operations of language: sensitivity to the meaning of words; to the order among words; to the sounds, rhythms, inflections and meters of words; and to language's ability to excite, convince, stimulate, convey information or please. A poet knows that *how* something is said is part of the message, probably the most important part. A poet works on the sounds and words until they communicate a newly discovered insight or offer a glimpse at a mystery. The words then capture the emotions that brought to life the desire to write the poem.

This intelligence is a hard one to value in a culture that jingleizes messages to make us purchase and consume, that fills the air around us with noise to keep us from knowing our own specific yearnings. It is an intelligence hard to value in a culture that embraces, as Stephen Dunn writes in *walking light*, "the capitalistic ethic of acquisition rather than contemplation, the celebration of things rather than soul."

But more and more, among writers, therapists, theologians and scholars, a correction to this problem is emerging. Julia Cameron's *The Artists' Way*, David Whyte's *The Heart Aroused* and Deena Metzger's *Writing for Your Life* are recent books on the topic of valuing contemplation as an extraordinary competency. To empower ourselves to write, we must search for support in valuing this intelligence and our practice of it, because our society has not valued this way of being and knowing the world. We are constantly asked to do, buy, go, behave, agree, imitate and envy. Who asks us "to be," "to explore our beings," "to treasure our insights?"

In order to empower ourselves to write poetry, we must refuse to see poetry as merely verse or ornament. We must refuse to see our linguistic intelligence as inferior or unworthy. We must refuse to let ourselves believe our feelings are inconsequential, or worse, wrong. In an essay called, "The Social Function of Poetry," T.S. Eliot said about the poet:

> . . . he is making people more aware of what they feel already, and therefore teaching them something about themselves. But he is not merely a more conscious person than the others; he is also individually different from other people, and from other poets too, and can make his readers share consciously in new feelings which they had not experienced before. That is the difference between the writer who is merely eccentric or mad and the genuine poet. The former may have feelings which are unique but which cannot be shared, and are therefore useless; the latter discovers new variations of sensibility which can be appropriated by others.

In his book *The Moment of Poetry*, Don Cameron Allen tells us we must operate from the understanding "that poetry is a form of knowledge and that the poet's mode of thinking is a valid means of understanding the mortal world."

This is hard, so we must create support for ourselves by joining or creating a poetry writing group, attending public readings of poetry, reading poets' work in books and magazines, and arranging space in our lives for the contemplation and perception that lead to writing poetry.

What does such an arrangement look like?

ARRANGE SPACE IN YOUR LIFE FOR THE CONTEMPLATION AND PERCEPTION WRITING POETRY REQUIRES

A place to write is important. Some of us require a whole room, others only a favorite spot by a window. Some of us start our work away from home in a café or parked in our cars where no one can interrupt us. Some of us need physical activity to jog our beings into rising clear of the chorus of errands and obligations. Provide yourself with a place to write, read or think; a way to transition to this place (running, biking, swimming, walking, preparing tea, gardening, showering, eating sweets); some regular time in your day, night or week to do this; and some supplies (books of poetry, paper, pens. I have never started a poem on the computer and I don't know anyone who has).

Don't get hung up on the place, time and supplies being perfect or "poetic." In fact, start without a huge investment that you must live up to or you may find yourself trapped. It is hard to write "well enough" to appease a capitalistic concern with materials, (for example, is my writing good enough for this fine leather-bound notebook?) It is just as hard to appease a preconceived notion about what is a spiritual or meaningful enough spot to be an okay writer's place. If you can only write where there are fresh flowers, white walls and total silence, you may be getting too out-of-this-world to include much of the world in your writing.

A spiral notebook, loose-leaf paper or legal pads and a Bic pen— or a free one from your bank, car dealer or insurance agent—will work just fine as long as they are there. Keep a regular writer's journal with you at all times, or just keep paper and pen in your car (those pads suction cupped to the dash work great, or use Post-its), near your bed and in your purse or briefcase (notebooks with covers are probably more useful here because they are sturdier). Once you decide to write poetry, lines and ideas arrive at the times you are least prepared to set them down. You must learn to accommodate their arrival.

Your poetry writing surroundings should be ones you are drawn to, not ones you engineer. Recently, I was shown the study of a wealthy woman who said she wanted to write but was having trouble starting. She had a separate stone cottage built as her writing studio after her professionally designed and decorated home was completed. Inside her studio, the shelves were completely bare except for a long-held collection of porcelain dolls! I wished that she had more of her ongoing life in her studio—the books she was reading, snapshots she enjoyed, monetarily valueless mementos of beach walks, a friend's gift of incense, dried roses or fall leaves; in other words, the company of a spare but friendly and idiosyncratic clutter.

If you are already writing, you have probably seen how the things you are intrigued with and that settle you down make their way into your writing spot the more you use it. I like to write at my grown daughter's old desk. I like looking at the windowsill where the stones my son collected as a little boy are displayed. I keep the painted fish my husband got from an international gift shop, announcing he liked the store so much that anyone was welcome anytime to get him anything from that store. I have a photograph of my friend's Buddha statue sitting among tulips in a Mt. Vernon field.

Of course, lots of times I have to get away from my writer's place to actually write. I have found that I can write in a Laundromat, but I can't write in trendy coffeehouses because the tables full of people furiously writing in their journals intimidates me. I feel like a kid in school during exams and achievement tests. Poet and doctor William Carlos Williams wrote in his car while parked outside patients' homes when he made house calls. Wherever you go to write, be sure to have one or two poetry books with you. Reading them will bring poetry to your doorstep.

Reading poems is a way of being among and listening to like-minded and like-hearted people. It is a way of filling yourself with the sounds of contemplation and the search for insight and knowing. It is a way of getting yourself to the place where you, too, are ready to speak and think that way.

Whatever time you schedule will work just fine, or if it wants to change, it will make you change it. Poetry works that way. It is the boss. Perhaps you have already found yourself scribbling at five o'clock each morning, or up later at night, or off in a sunny corner during lunch at work, or stopping by a lake in a park between errands or after work.

You might find yourself organizing your weekends differently and relishing twenty-four hours with no commitments other than writing. Art often comes to us after we have been working to dig it out of ourselves and have given up, left our desk and gone to relax. Find some time when you can feel your way into these transitions between trying hard and relaxing, rather than having them imposed by others' demands and schedules. Insight does come concerning the life questions we are asking, but to get it, you might need to be alone. When you are alone, you stand a better chance of attaching to what Richard Hugo called a "triggering" subject. For Hugo, the triggering subject was often a town he was new to. For others, it is an object, an expression on someone's face, the sound of something or a particular taste. Whatever causes you to start writing, describing the triggering subject will help you find your real subject.

Wanting to write and giving yourself space and permission to do so are not enough in themselves. You must be confident that you will follow through with the writing no matter how bad you think your beginning efforts are. In fact, you must begin with the idea that there is no "bad" writing, that all first efforts and even many revisions create the opportunity for good writing.

NURTURE THE CONFIDENCE AND STRENGTH TO START WRITING POETRY

Here are eleven actions you can perform to help yourself feel solid about beginning to write poetry and sticking to it:
- You do not have to tell anyone you are doing this.
- You do not have to justify it, even to yourself.
- You must not judge anything that you are writing as worthy or unworthy.
- You must keep writing.
- Do not whine about not having enough time or energy to write; do not think that only under altered circumstances would you be able to write. Instead, go and write, and go and write some more; your circumstances will alter themselves.
- Do not tell yourself you are a bad writer, a dilettante or lacking wisdom.
- Tell yourself you are committed to writing, and to letting the words and craft help you see and understand.
- Read what poets have said about writing. (See the appendices.)
- Keep a notebook of your favorite quotes from this reading. Post the quotes on the wall where you write or tape them to your desk.

- Notice the good press poetry is getting: articles in newspapers about poets, programs on National Public Television, appointments of state and national poet laureates, impressive anthologies at bookstores.
- Notice how good you feel after you have written or spent even a few minutes reading a poem. Remember this feeling.

INTO THE ABYSS OF THE UNKNOWN WHERE DISCOVERIES AND TRUTHS ARE FOUND

In the July/August 1996 edition of *Poets & Writers Magazine*, Samuel Hazo tells us that "thought and feeling interpenetrate one another constantly." We must put, he says, what the famous French philosopher and theologian Jacques Maritain called "intelligenciated sense" into our words. He states, "There is no question that the language of 'felt thought' must be quarried from our personal depths. Like the best gold, it does not lie on the surface." Whether we say that poems put our senses into our thinking or intelligence into our senses, we cannot usually create this enriched combination without performing the deep quarrying Hazo mentions.

But this quarrying frightens us. Why?

First, we are taught to wait and speak only when our feelings cool, and we think we can speak reasonably. Quarrying ourselves for felt thoughts certainly breaks this cool and heats us up again. How do we know we can manage the chaos of heated language? We fear being overcome by it. We fear breaking a norm to which we have been socialized.

We are taught that when we want to speak with feeling, sentimental greeting cards suffice. We are conditioned to believe there is no need to find our own way of precisely conveying what we feel. To quarry ourselves for that precise feeling would be beside the point, we may think. I'm not special. I have no special way of seeing or speaking. Who am I to go after such a thing? Who would want to hear "confessional" poetry as it was dubbed years back? The personal does not have to be merely private. The personal in poetry is the transpersonal. What you have experienced and where you have found mystery or wisdom can be conveyed through poetry that offers others the experience you had and releases it in the shape of that poetry, the discovery you made, your knowing.

William Matthews explained that the photographer Diane Arbus began her career thinking that to be universal, she would have to photograph only the nonpersonal—stones, trees. But as she explored her art, she began to take more idiosyncratic photographs. Her fame is built upon photos of particular, peculiar people. This work is universal. By photographing these people as she saw them, she shared the universal. Her audience can see the pain, sorrow, fear and detachment in themselves when they view these photographs.

We are taught to generalize and abstract, and that to sound objective is to sound wise. But these are only more defenses against entering the quarry. And we pay for not entering. As Hazo says, "When a word misses the mark, the feeling remains in limbo." When we do not speak from feelings and sensations filtered through our unique beings in relation to the tangible world, we are likely to find that our feelings appear quite askew in the form of hysterical outbursts, inappropriate giggling and even violence.

In writing poetry, these skewed emotions appear when we have not been able to fully rappel into the quarry. There are language equivalents of hysteria, giggling and violence, and I will discuss them and show you examples. Since this descent into the abyss is so difficult, the best we can do as writers is to learn to recognize where the skewed emotions are showing up in our poems in progress and begin to make them straight. These places of skewed emotions show us where we need to mine, bringing more experience to light. These places are platforms for the next trip down.

Although finished poems look as if they were effortlessly composed at one sitting with no seams showing, the poem is actually something ventured for over time. As I said in the introduction, Louise Glück describes writing poems as beginning with a haunting, as if the finished poem already exists somewhere.

To write the poem, to find the shape and form of the experience that haunts you, you must keep rappelling into the abyss and mining for the experience. In these searches, all you have to go on are the clues left where the writing went awry.

NOTICE WHERE THE WRITING GOES AWRY

Here are examples culled from some students' works in progress. The examples have no names attached because they are only the beginnings. They are the kind of perfectly respectable works in progress we must all learn to accept as we start. They are words committed to the page that capture as closely as the writers could describe what they were finding on their first expeditions. Now the writers' work is to recognize where they must venture further. They can do this by understanding the emotionally masking qualities of sing-songy, chimey sounds; terribly mixed metaphors; overly certain tones and mixed diction; and an overabundance of Latinate abstract words.

Sing-Songy, Chimey Sounds

This poem was written to a friend who had told the poet about a dream she had.

Sprung

Throw it down now
that rusted, toothless saw
you used to hide beneath you
while in your dreams
winged creatures (now extinct)
chased and taunted you
with bully threats.
The bars have vanished
like a fairy after favoring
one dearest wish.

Take the next few
fearful steps alone,
she would have urged.
The earth will awaken
to the kiss of your feet.
And heed, if on the path
appears a ghostly gate
then lift your heart and
let your arms swing past it.

In the strident, sing-songy rhythm of the last six lines, you can hear that the poet feels certain she can give good advice to the friend. Each of these lines has six stressed syllables in a row except one that has five, which is close enough to the established beat not to change the rhythm. In these six lines, the line breaks make us expect rhymes in alternating lines. "Feet" and "gate" rhyme. The lines ending in "awaken," "path" and "and" all have "a" sounds in them. The rhyme and meter are very regular as is the sound of certainty.

However, when someone else's dream makes you want to write, the poem that will have the most meaning is the one that shares your own experience, not the poem that repossesses the friend's dream and spits it out as your authoritative experience.

If this were my work in progress, I would note that the sound shows the certainty that I want to speak to my friend. I would rewrite the inverted language to read more naturally: "If a ghostly gate / appears on your path, lift / your heart and let your / arms swing past it." I would listen to the difference in sound. I would go back with the gentler sound in my ears and try to find my true voice on the subject, not my teacherly, certain, it's-all-sewed-up sounding voice.

Terribly Mixed Metaphors

Once I had converted that line to regular speech, I would notice some confusion. "Lift your heart," it says, and then goes on to say "let your arms swing past it." "Lift your heart" is a version of the expressions "our hearts were lifted," "he lifted my heart," "my heart lifted when. . . ." But the command to lift your heart is somehow different. The you in the poem would need tools, and arms and hands to use the tools. So when the arms "swing past it," I see a heart thrown up and falling to the ground. I know it is not what the writer meant, but in our language, the "it" refers more to the heart than the gate. These are busy arms. In the inverted, strident language, this confusion was not as glaring, but it is there. If the writing makes our literal selves confused or amused where the poet wants us to feel deeply, we cannot enter the world of the poem. I would see that the arms are replacing and distracting me from imagery that would be useful to making the exploration the poem requires. The arms are trying to be a shortcut to evoking the experience of only pausing by that ghostly gate, of not letting the ghostly qualities get the you down. *Okay*, I would say to myself, *I can't feel my heart or the you's heart lift, or myself or the you swing past the gate until I really know what that gate is and why I called it a ghostly gate.* I would write about what I meant by that gate, or what had happened when I or the you went in.

Overly Certain Tones and Mixed Diction

"The bars have vanished / like a fairy after favoring / one dearest wish." Don't fairy godmothers usually *grant* rather than *favor* a wish?

This word seems odd here. What does favor mean here? That the fairy decided which wish of several to grant? Who was that fairy, what was the wish she favored, and what were the other possible wishes?

"The bars have vanished like a fairy." Why haven't they vanished like a stain under cleanser or a car at an intersection or clouds when a storm breaks? Is this like Hansel in the cage getting plump for good eating? But as I remember, it was Gretel's cleverness that got Hansel out, not a fairy. What does the writer get from introducing the fairy?

I think the diction is serving the writer's desire to be the one that knows what the fairy would have said if there were a fairy. This piece is filled with imperatives and knowledge of what is true for the you though we don't know how the speaker got this knowledge. The imperatives are "throw it down," "take the next few steps," "lift your heart," "let your arms swing." The knowledge reported is "the bars have vanished like a fairy after favoring one wish," "the earth will awaken," "it will be safe." How does the writer know this? From what personal experience?

If this were my poem in progress, I'd notice the oddness of the word "favor" and let my thoughts about it recenter me in the work. I like the image of the rusted, toothless saw hidden beneath the you while winged creatures chase and taunt bully threats, but I would decide that the winged creatures are enough of a fairy tale reference and I'd move to newer, fresher images. I'd make that saw my own. Perhaps I'd say, "I take the rusted, toothless saw you used to hide beneath you while winged creatures chased and taunted bully threats." Now I'd have challenged myself to say what I'd do with it. Where would I go with it? Behind the ghostly gate? Could the gate be not ghostly but real now that I realized that leaning on these fairy tale images kept me from writing my experience?

Latinate Abstract Words

Here is a first effort from another student:

> Look at me! Hear me! I have food for this need.
> Thought food, soul food
> Sustenance for a romp with muses
> Who heed these phrases of joy and doubt
> Wrapped in plain detail and utter repose
> All the flaws and miracles that are we.

"Thought," "soul," "sustenance," "joy," "doubt." These five abstract words appear in three consecutive lines. When this writer says, "Look at me! Hear me! I have food for this need," I am all eyes, all ears. I want to see the food she has, and smell it, taste it, chew it, digest it. But she lets me down when she calls it "thought food, soul food" as if that is enough. I'm being called to an empty table and told to pretend I am eating. I am disappointed.

The writing opportunity here is to make me heed the "flaws and miracles that we are" by giving me the actual detail, not telling me it will be wrapped in detail. Roll up the sleeves and say, okay, I will cook this meal, I will package it as a picnic for the muses, I will present it on a blanket, in a meadow of glacier lilies, on a day in early spring when I have hiked to see these flowers that bloom only a short while.

This writer has the confidence to say the muses heed the phrases, but she didn't act from her confidence. Oops! Well, that happens sometimes. Allowing oneself to write poems is not easy. The knowledge that she feels confident is all she needs to go back into the quarry and find the food to nurture the muses!

RISK ENCOUNTERING YOUR DEEPEST, TRUEST FEELING

It is not easy at first to recognize the ways emotions have appeared askew in your work in progress. Let time go by between first drafts and revisions because the longer you are away from your initial words, the more open-minded you can be upon relistening. Find an interested listener or group of poem makers and begin sharing your drafts to get a sense of what words and sounds move or distance your listeners.

But most importantly, learn to let the words and lines you write take you into the abyss where chaos must reign for a while, and where you risk encountering your deepest, truest feelings.

Here are some hints to help you do this:

1. Make a point to get comfortable in the abyss. As David Rigsbee said at the Summer 1996 Centrum Writer's Conference, "Life is a pulse, an out and an in. Expansion; contraction. . . . An answer is death, closure; it forecloses on other options." If you have difficulty in the chaos, remember Rigsbee's idea of pulse and let new words breathe oxygen into your draft. Take out other words here and there, and see if a contraction helps.

2. Write with your ear as much as with your eyes and heart. In *The Third Ear: On Listening to the World*, author and jazz enthusiast

Joachim-Ernst Berendt wrote: "Someone listening . . . takes in, dissolving separation. Hearing disperses isolation." Listen to the sound of what you are writing and keep listening for more of it.

3. Do not judge what you write with the logical mind just yet. What may seem to be opposites may in fact be parts of a whole. You will find out when you climb out of the abyss—the place you have gone because you don't yet know what you are thinking and must discover it.

4. Use metaphor, analogy and associations. This is the kind of thinking that allows your mind to move and not get stymied.

5. Keep writing and accepting the words and images that come to you without imposing ideas of how your writing should be—your felt thought will arise from your experience and, therefore, will bear the exact images of your experience and not empty symbols merely borrowed from the culture. When you judge, you may choose words you think are better but are not from direct experience. In revising, you may have to comb through for such "empty" words and get back into the experience for fresher imagery.

6. The struggle to overcome the personality's wish to control and direct the outcomes of your experience makes hanging out in the chaotic abyss of not-knowing so uncomfortable. Talk to your personality. Tell it you admire its skill, the way it gets you through a day and builds a social world for you. But right now, WRITE now, feed your wish to know experience without agenda. You must write in order to recreate experience itself.

7. Remember that the words of the material and natural, sensual world are the materials for the soul's exploration of experience. Use the names of plants, animals, geographies, places, products and people, the colors, sounds, tastes and smells that come to you when you immerse yourself in the world. The soul thrives and comes to power in this specificity, not in the abstractions and sanitized language we have learned to lean on in academic and business writing and even in reporting.

8. Remember the power of lists. When you feel overcome by disorder, let the structure of lists keep you calm. The soul does not rebel too much if the items on the list are interesting. For instance, if you are writing out of strong feelings for your mother, list what you remember about her voice, including the exact words she spoke to you over the years. What do you remember about her clothes? Name them— springulator pumps; yellow-and-white polka-dot wraparound shifts; a

gray, Persian lamb's wool coat. What do you remember about the gifts she gave? The guitar you wanted but cost more than she wanted to pay. The small plastic doll, bought at a train station, no taller than your five-year-old hand, with the silky hair and the hairbrush to brush it with. The wooden-handled, stainless steel cheese spreader from Denmark that you didn't know what to do with at twenty-three, but at forty-nine find you love with a tenderness that is hard to bear and may stand for all the ways you didn't recognize love. What do you remember about her interests? Flour spread over the countertop when she baked, the voices of women playing cards as you drifted to sleep, how she sat in a beach chair with one knee up to her chin? Precision with images and details are the playground of the soul. Each leads to others and before you know it, you are more comfortable in this experiencing of experience without trying to control it. It will eventually show you the shape it is working toward. You will see it.

ENCOURAGE THE POETRY WRITING SPELL

Many writers know when a poem is arriving by the sounds or images that come to them. They may feel that the world looks more vivid; that meaningful words, phrases and events come to them syncronistically from the world around them (as if the poet had a hook or a net or a magnet out for them). Some report hearing lines. Others report a body sensation of impressions that come from associations between what they are experiencing now and what they have remembered from the past. They know they want their pad and pen.

Learn to come to these associations, vivid sensings and suddenly heard words with what Mary Oliver calls the "purposeful part" of your writing self, which must meet the "wild, silky part of ourselves" as serious as Romeo was each time he met Juliet. Do not ignore these words and impressions. Transcribe them as much as you can.

WRITE EVEN WHEN THE SPELL IS BROKEN

Philip Levine once recounted at a festival in Seattle that he wrote a whole series of poems by living in his bed for a week. The writing ended, he said, the day his wife suddenly changed his sheets while he was in the bathroom.

Many writers feel they must not change a thing in their environment when they are at work. But the world has a way of intruding: it's dinnertime and we must prepare food for our family; it's time to get back to our jobs; we made a plan with someone and they're at our front door; we are writing in our car and the sun goes down. The spell is broken. How do we begin again?

We must make and keep appointments with ourselves to write. The more we do this, the more our unconscious comes forward. We create the place for this to happen, both physically and mentally.

We must often reorient ourselves to the sound of poetry. Reread what you have written at your last sitting. Read other poets' work before you start to write.

And some of us have found help by eating chocolate just before we write. Yeats said that to write one must always be a little bit in love. The digestion of chocolate releases the same chemicals in the brain that infatuation releases!

Think of what you love: the dandelion growing in the dry, rough gravel by the driveway; the way your daughter's eyebrows knit together when she is concentrating; the circle of jam around her mouth; those good and lazy mornings in the summer; the familiar feel of your wool knit cap on your forehead in winter. Make a detailed list. This will reawaken your poetry writing mind.

Do poetry writing exercises (there are many in chapters four and five and in books listed in the appendices). They keep your mind working in a way that is receptive to the part of yourself Mary Oliver says "brings the heat of the star as opposed to the shape of a star."

Even if you think you have nothing to say, write for at least half the time you sit in your writing spot. Writing poetry often has nothing to do with what you think you have to say anyway. The words in your poetry most often appear by surprise. Remember: Writer's write. They exercise the writing muscle just to keep it toned. Better writing comes from just writing. It is amazing how many wonderful lines and stanzas I have found in my early notes. Earlier in my writing life, I didn't know what I was dealing with or how to deal with it. Years down the road, I am prepared with more skill and a better developed ear.

◆ ◆ ◆

You have now begun to prepare the physical and emotional geography and climate for your poetry writing. Next, we will look more closely at how reading poetry can help you write poems. Then we'll explore strategies for beginning poems that may surprise you and make you feel you are magically pulling poems out of a hat. This is good. All poems are magic, a surprise, the appearance of something that was not there before!

CHAPTER THREE

Reading Poetry for Help Writing Poems

You should be reading poetry constantly just to see what you can learn from other poets.
—David Kirby
Writing Poetry

Poets read poetry. They like the way it sounds; they like what it addresses. They read it in libraries and bookstores, at magazine stands and newsstands. They subscribe to literary magazines, have friends and families who give them poetry collections and buy poetry books for themselves. They type poems out for their friends, read them on their friends' voice mail, and, thanks to arts commission-funded poetry-in-motion projects, notice them on bus and subway placards. Poets keep track of new collections by poets they admire. They read reviews of poetry books in *The New York Times Book Review* and other literary reviews. They sometimes savor reading poetry, sometimes gorge on it, sometimes sneak it a little bit at a time, sometimes offer a taste of it to someone else and sometimes hoard it for awhile. Reading poetry is as much a part of a poet's week as cooking, grocery shopping, watching TV, doing the laundry, exercising and holding down a job.

Poets learn from other poets because they use the same way of thinking to explore life, and truth in poetry gives poets permission to find truth in their own poems.

If you have not yet begun reading as much contemporary poetry (which is best for exploring personal poetry) as you should, you may be consciously or unconsciously worrying that poems must always have full rhymes in couplets or in alternating lines of a stanza. You may think the best poetry comes in forms you never quite think in—sonnets, sestinas, ballads. You may think of great literature that uses outdated language full of word order inversions and odd phrasings to make the rhymes possible and wonder if you need to use diction like that. You may think of the sacred literature you have studied and wonder if it is really okay to write poems about the everyday. We will look at one old-fashioned poem and three contemporary poems, one of which is in a form called the pantoum. We'll see how language and diction work to impart the emotional message of each poem. We will see that old-fashioned devices are not necessary today, though they worked in their own day, and that free verse offers a richness of form that propels the poet's search for epiphany. Finally, even in form, contemporary poets strive to make the form not call attention to itself.

If you have been reading contemporary poems and think you are not quite "getting" them, you may be wondering what makes them poems when they seem like ordinary speech. If you have felt the urgency and angst in contemporary poems, you might remain unconvinced that you can write strong poems from your own experience, from your own times.

To overcome both of these dilemmas, you must get the sound of contemporary poets in your ear and differentiate their sound from that of earlier English poetry. Read the poetry of current times as well as essays on poetry and writing poetry by today's poets. The appendices include the books I have learned from and enjoyed reading as well as the names of literary magazines that publish fine contemporary poetry and reviews of poets' work. As I continue to discuss contemporary poetry, I'll quote from the poets whose writing on poetry has informed me. It would be worth your while to read these poets' words on poetry in full.

THE GOAL OF READING POETRY

John Ciardi had a knack for writing about the way to read poetry. In *Mid-Century American Poets*, the poetry anthology he edited in 1950, Ciardi wrote a thorough and inspiring introduction in which he asks and answers the question, "What does it take to read a poem?" Modern poetry, he said, is "unfamiliar and tentative," with no final judges; therefore, he said to read poems for delight. Instead of *forcing* the poem to make sense, realize the "poem *is* sense. The kind of communication that happens in a poem is infinitely closer to that of music than to that of prose," he wrote.

In 1959, Ciardi went further with his discussion in a book called *How a Poem Means*. He found that asking, "How does a poem mean?" is more useful than asking, "What does a poem mean?" He said it was worth finding out how a poem "built itself into a form out of images, ideas, and rhythms" and "how these elements become the meaning and are inseparable from it." He said that first you enjoy a poem just for the sounds and rhythms of it, with no thoughtful activity. The next level is where pleasure lies in overcoming difficulties. For the poet, that pleasure "lies in overcoming meaningful and thoughtful (and 'feelingful') difficulties, and for the reader in identifying with the poet in that activity."

The goal of reading poetry is not to define it, but to experience what it offers. If we can do this, Ciardi says, there is a step beyond, where "there inevitably arrives a sense that one is also experiencing himself as a human being." The more we can experience ourselves as human beings in the reading of others' poetry, the more we can realize ourselves as human beings in our own poems.

Paul Valéry agreed. "When a poem compels one to read it with passion, . . . the reader feels he is 'momentarily its author,' " and "that is how he knows the poem is beautiful." Reading and writing poetry are two lanes on the same street.

SAMPLE POEMS FOR STUDY

Following is a guided reading of four American poems. My discussion of them will help you learn how to receive the emotional and literal information that poems deliver.

Before we get to the three contemporary poems—one each by three of my teachers: Stephen Dunn, William Matthews and Nelson Bentley—consider the following excerpt from a poem written by early American settler Anne Bradstreet, one of the first significant American poets. We will see that how we read a poem, though influenced by the diction of the poet's times or by the poet's use of a formal pattern, is the same for contemporary free verse as for structured classical forms.

On June 23, 1659, Anne Bradstreet is thinking about her children, grown and away from home. She is thinking of them as birds who have taken flight:

> My age I will not once lament,
> But sing, my time so near is spent.

And from the top bough take my flight
Into a country beyond sight,
Where old ones instantly grow young,
And there with seraphims set song;
No seasons cold, nor storms they see;
But spring lasts to eternity.
When each of you shall in your nest
Among your young ones take your rest,
In chirping language, oft them tell,
You had a dam that loved you well,
That did what could be done for young,
And nursed you up till you were strong,
And 'fore she once would let you fly,
She showed you joy and misery;
Taught what was good, and what was ill,
What would save life, and what would kill.
Thus gone, amongst you I may live,
And dead, yet speak, and counsel give:
Farewell, my birds, farewell adieu,
I happy am, if well with you.

What is left for a mother bird once her young have started nests of their own? To sing, to fly. Anne Bradstreet says she will sing and not lament until she dies, and she sees death as a flight into another world of eternal spring and youth. She imagines her bird-children singing in their nests to their bird-children, telling them about their grandmother and the intelligence and care with which she raised her young. This gives the poet comfort because in that way she will still be among the ones she loves. Arriving at that place of comfort through an act of her imagination, she is able to say, "I happy am, if well with you." Here is an achievement of unselfish letting go, of coming to terms with time and its way of taking away what we love though it is unable to take it away completely. What seems incomplete and full of loss becomes, through the poem's sound and images, holographic, with love re-forming itself whole and complete.

The poem works emotionally though it is old-fashioned in its devices. Word order is sometimes altered to fit the regular rhyme scheme. Each line has the same regular rhythm (stressed and unstressed syllables), and almost every line is stopped by punctuation.

This stopping of the lines makes the reader pause and consider the particular thought in the preceding phrase, seeing it as a whole. This rhetorical form is like a hologram: Look at each line separately, and see a complete lesson about love. The more holograms of love we see, the more we experience its undying strength.

Now let's look at a poem by a father, Stephen Dunn, which was written upon his daughter's birth. It appears in his 1976 collection *Full of Lust and Good Usage*. As you read it, be aware of the ways in which you think the poem is "gaining pounds," making it, as Stanley Plumly taught in his classes, something that "weighs more at the bottom than at the top."

> *Waiting With Two Members of a Motorcycle*
> *Gang for My Child to Be Born*
> for Andrea

> I was talking to "The Eliminators"
>   when you were born,
> two of them, high as slag heaps and
>   uncles to be,
> all in black for the occasion.
>   All you wanted was out;
> you couldn't have known that you
>   were "Life"
> when you came, or that your father
>   was let loose
> from graduate school, a believer
>   in symbols.
> I expected "The Eliminators" to
>   disappear, snuffed out
> by a stronger force, a white tornado
>   of my own.
> That's not what happens, though,
>   in life
> as you will learn. They smiled when
>   they heard of you
> and shook my hand. At another time
>   it might

have been my head. May you turn
   stone, my daughter,
into silk. May you make men better
   than they are.

In this seemingly direct poem, Stephen Dunn is following advice he gave students in his university classroom. He had written the following quotation on the blackboard:

> As Wei T'ai said in the 11th C, be precise about the thing, reticent about the feeling. Modesty is being truthful, genuine. By walking on surfaces, we get to the center of our poems. Poems are love's bleeding and its healing, a form of letting.

Certainly one way his poem performs is with both reticence and precision. The motorcycle gang the men belong to has a name: The Eliminators. The speaker of the poem has a role: He is a graduate student who is away from classes during the birth of his daughter. The speaker knows he is in a different sociological group than the other men waiting there. He feels they might on another day hurt him, kill him, do away with life rather than congratulate its arrival. The speaker confronts the truth he addresses to his daughter: idealized versions of the world—where good overcomes evil, where education overcomes brute destructive force—are not accurate visions. The speaker is modest and truthful about his awkwardness among these men "high as slag heaps." Dunn's poem walks on the surfaces of his moment: the hospital waiting room, the people in the room, the notion of where he has just come from. He walks with these images and details toward his daughter's birth. He brings them all to her with the poem, with the prayer born of this poem's moment that her spirit may be capable of turning stone into silk, capable of making "men better than they are." Already this daughter has been a portent of good luck: The threatening men have shaken the poet's hand, not his head, and they have smiled, not glared. In the sound of the ending, we hear the poet humbly praying that having a daughter will make him better than he is and be a passage for him in his life. Here the poem weighs the most because resonating with the lessons of this life is this moment of honest, personal evaluation, aspiration and hope.

How a poem sounds is a big part of how a poem means. Until the last sentence of this poem, there is a preponderance of "o" and double "o" sounds. This is soothing, soft. A father, less than heroic, welcomes his new daughter to the world, less than ideal though it is.

> . . . At another time
>   it might
> have been my head. May you turn
>   stone, my daughter,
> into silk. May you make men better
>   than they are.

"Might" has an internal "i" sound that rhymes with "time" at the end of the preceding line. "Stone" has an internal vowel rhyme with "turn" at the end of the preceding line. "Silk" and "daughter" do not rhyme, so my ear feels a bit let down and still expects one, but when the last line says, "May you make men better / than they are," my ear also hears "better than their ilk." A silly chimey rhyme that the poet had the good sense to turn down, but that good sense also tells us something about the emotional truth of the poem. If he had used a word like ilk, he would have been distancing himself from men by using a judging, categorizing, editorial kind of word and showing himself to be above the rest. With the word "are" he is using a form of the verb "to be" that lends itself to inclusion—he is. In his "isness" he is a man, and may his daughter make men—all men, but particularly her father—better than they are.

In contemporary poetry, a poem about the hallowed birth of a child including images of motorcycle gang members is not unusual. A poet often uses the images and details that surround him or her during a time of publicly acknowledged great importance to find out the unique inner importance of the moment. These images and details are part of the truth of the moment, and the literalness of that truth helps the poem by the end to mean more than the sum of its parts.

Another of my teachers, William Matthews, spent time as a single parent to two sons. One of my favorites among his poems is from his 1973 volume, *Rising and Falling*.

Bedtime

Usually I stay up late, my time
alone. Tonight at 9:00 I can tell
I'm only awake long enough
to put my sons to bed.
When I start to turn off lights
the boys are puzzled. They're used
to entering sleep by ceding to me
their hum and fizz, the way they give me
50 to hold so they can play
without money. I'm their night-light.
The bread baked while they sleep.
And I can scarcely stand up, dry
in the mouth and dizzied
by fatigue. From our rooms
we call back and forth the worn
magic of our passwords and let one
another go. In the morning Sebastian
asks who was the last to fall
asleep and none of us cares or knows.

In William Matthews' class, I learned that the insides of the words in a poem must form a common landscape and not clash. What are the insides of words? I guess one way to think of them is as voices inside words, like the voices of the toys that come to life in the film *Toy Story*; voices that call to each other across the corridors that separate words in a poem, like the boys and their father call in the dark from separate rooms. These voices must form a community of conversation and background, a kind of landscape that can absorb the highs and lows, thuds and whispers as if they all belonged there.

This father sets up his occasion for this poem: He is so tired that he begins turning out lights on his way to bed. He metaphorically names what he is to his boys: "their night-light. The bread baked while they sleep." These words build a domestic landscape even though one word is for something mechanical and the other for something organic. Isn't parenting composed of both the mechanical and the organic? Some problems are worked out and some activities performed by rote, while other actions and solutions come from particular moments that grow as yeast grows in bread. This calling out of names before sleep is a new action born of the father lying down at the same time as his boys. Isn't it both an organic solution the organism of the family creates as well as a rote use of energy in its repetition?

Inside the poem, other words form a landscape, or a community of voices as I think of them: the boys have fizz associated with them; the father dizziness. Using internal rhyme, these words form a community. The word "fall" ends a line; that is what release into separateness can feel like and reading the line, we fall with the word momentarily forgetting it is part of the phrase "fall asleep." But we are caught again at the beginning of the next line by the word "asleep"—"asleep and none of us cares or knows." It is morning now. Night and morning are not the same—different landscapes, different emotions, different cares, different concerns. Fizz in the boys and no dizziness in Dad.

I hope you are beginning to see the ways that poems embody feeling and offer the experience of a feeling inseparable from the poet's particular words and the way they are put together.

We'll move on to a poem in form (a pantoum with lines repeated in a particular pattern) by Nelson Bentley upon watching his ten-year-old daughter play the zither. It appeared in his 1977 collection, *Moose Call.*

Julian at Ten

Snow comes down, a multitude in feather
Across the valley, snow fills every pine.
Julian sits improvising on her zither,
Under a wallhanging of the tree of life.

Across the valley, snow fills every pine.
Faith and joy have always been my weather.
Under a wallhanging of the tree of life,
I have become the archetypal father.

Faith and joy have always been my weather:
Devoted but eccentric as they come,
I have become the archetypal father.
She tells her innocence with finger and thumb.

Devoted but eccentric as they come,
I watch the past reborn in my daughter.
She tells her innocence with finger and thumb.
Bookcases of poets listen to her zither.

I watch the past reborn in my daughter;
All day her sled has coasted Fritz's hill.
Bookcases of poets listen to her zither.
In her my mother plays the piano still.

All day her sled has coasted Fritz's hill;
Last night we laughed over Mark Twain's burglar.
In her my mother plays the piano still.
We are enclosed in love as by a blizzard.

Last night we laughed over Mark Twain's burglar.
The zither finds her happiness a tune:
We are enclosed in love as by a blizzard.
Beth's dark intensity is in her frown.

The zither finds her happiness a tune.
Twirling her hair, she tells herself a story:
Beth's dark intensity is in her frown.
The future is turning into history.

Twirling her hair, she tells herself a story:
Imagination illuminates our home.
The future is turning into history.
Maybe tonight we'll play a game of carom.

Imagination illuminates our home;
Julian sits improvising on her zither.
Maybe tonight we'll play a game of carom.
Snow comes down, a multitude in feather.

"Evoke, don't state." These were among the many dictates
Nelson Bentley drilled into his students. "Compression is the first
grace of style." "Poetry is the clear expression of mixed emotions."
"Art builds toward culmination of insight."

Here is a poem in which we certainly experience art building to insight. The first line is lovely as we read it, "Snow comes down, a multitude in feather." How complicated the patterns of each airy snowflake. How ample the number of flakes that form a snowstorm! How complex the pantoum form. (The pantoum is a Malayan form in which lines two and four of each stanza are repeated in lines one and three of the next stanza and so on.) How ample the lines become in their repetitions and new placements. By the time we read the first line again at the poem's end, "the multitude in feather" is far more than snow—Julian improvises on a zither after sledding all day. Small and surrounded by bookcases full of poets, she might seem like a feather fluttered down from the past as it flies into the future. She contains in herself the poet's mother playing the piano, the poet's wife's dark intensity and the imagination of her father. She is the seed and root of her father's archetypal fatherhood. She is part of the tree of life represented on the wallhanging above her.

With the phrase "faith and joy," we hear Christmas in the background of the poet's feelings and associations as Julian tells her innocence, just as the poet must recall a boyhood innocence once associated with Christmas. We feel as if we know this house with the snow and trees outside, the zither and wallhanging and bookcases inside, the father and daughter sharing Mark Twain, imagination and poetry.

But poetry is the clear expression of mixed emotions: She is also herself, a young daughter with whom he might play a game of carom on this night that he also sees all that she means to him. The mix of the archetypal and the everyday heightens the insight the poet is experiencing this particular evening about his deep joy and the poignancy of fatherhood, about life and its generational stream.

Whether you have experienced parenthood from both the child and the parent sides or only from the child side, these poems should resonate with you because they are truthful and universal, though idiosyncratic in their journeys. The children make a difference in their fathers' lives and create a passage and an internal humbling. The fathers pause—one in a hospital waiting room with motorcycle gang members, one in bed in a house of dark bedrooms and another in a living room one afternoon after his daughter's sledding—and use the images of the occasions that propelled them to write. The lyric or timeless quality of the poems comes from the sounds of common language.

If you are literal about your surroundings during occasions when you are moved to write, a lot of the work of poem writing will be done. The next work of the poet is to hear the insides of the words and find the landscape they want to hang around in, the reason they have come together. Then the poet helps the words grow a body, whether in form or free verse.

◆ ◆ ◆

Let's look at some of the tools and strategies a poet uses. In the next two chapters, a number of exercises will introduce tools and strategies you can use to begin poems. Do these exercises, and you will have a batch of work ready for developing in chapters six through nine.

CHAPTER FOUR

Practice With Tools for Poetry Writing

Only after looking and listening
 closely
can one make these various subtleties
 work magic.
 —*from Lu Chi's* Wen Fu,
 translated by Sam Hamill

Sometimes a poet thinks, "I am going to write a series of poems about my father," or "Now is a good time to write love poems to my new wife or husband or lover." But more often, a poet is suddenly overcome with the feeling that they must write because a detail or mood connected to a detail sticks like a cactus needle in their consciousness. They are compelled to explore this "soul puncture" in the form of a poem. To be up to this sort of exploration means recognizing a puncture has occurred, being equipped with tools for the coming exploration and having previous experience using the tools.

You must savor the peculiar persistent feeling that nags at you and puts particular words in your head. Then you must honor the recognition by committing these words to the page as well as whatever other words follow.

After this, the exploration begins. To go further, you need to know how 1) to use images and metaphors, 2) to hear the sound of your writing voice, and 3) to discard discordant diction and detail. Writing for practice from exercises proposed by a teacher or writing colleague is a way to learn these three things.

When I think of poetry writing practice, I think of my husband playing miniature golf with me so I could practice putting and not get bored. I think of an outdoor equipment company in my city that built an indoor mountain in their new store for people to learn and practice climbing. Here are opportunities to practice parts of the real thing without the need to do other parts: in the case of putting practice, not needing to drive; in the case of climbing practice, not needing to travel or negotiate the weather.

Writing poems from poetry exercises is a form of practice offered under safe and defined conditions. Paradoxically, in the case of writing from exercises, the better the writing practice goes, the more the poet writes to the place where (because he or she is not being careful to avoid feelings) that cactus needle jumps out and lodges in the skin. (I am thinking, by the way, of the jumping chollah cactus, which grows in Arizona.)

In poetry writing practice, you begin to use the tools of the craft. You also begin to train your ears, eyes, and heart to locate where the cactus needle has lodged in you and from where it has jumped. The following exercises will help you gain experience using these tools. Then by reading the work of students who did these exercises and my discussions of their work in the following chapters, you will begin to train your ears, eyes and heart. You will learn to recognize the poems that may be jumping out at you and how to craft them.

LISTS

In a well-known poem, "Things to Do Around a Lookout," poet and naturalist Gary Snyder listed things he could do while working for the forest service as a lookout for fires. He spent a lot of time alone in the small quarters, and his poem details life there by listing actions he could take and objects he could use. Among my favorites are airing out musty sleeping bags, bathing in snow melt, the star book and the rock book, oolong sapchong tea, and putting salt out for the ptarmigan.

Many poems are lists. Many lists survive inside poems. As an exercise, listing gives you practice using exact names and characteristics. It gives you an opportunity to dredge up subjects containing that cactus needle. The only trick is figuring out a list that interests you. Here are some ideas to get you started. List:

- Seven or more things you see outside a window right now that someone else might not notice
- Seven or more jobs you think you'd like and describe in detail what you would wear to each of them

- Seven or more things that are in your refrigerator and why they are there
- Seven or more gifts you have been given, when and by whom
- Seven or more occasions when you wished you could disappear; name names, places and actions by you or others
- Seven or more lies you have told, to whom and when
- Seven or more compliments you have given, to whom and when
- Seven or more ways you would curse someone who has angered you
- Seven or more ways you have been complimented and by whom
- Seven people you think of right now and why you are thinking of them
- Seven or more songs you know and what people, places or events they make you think of
- Seven titles of more lists you could make

Challenge yourself to write one of these lists each day. When you have tried all of them, do some over again. Enough time will have passed that you will think of something different to list. Keep your lists in a journal or box, or on your computer. Read them from time to time to remind yourself that you have a unique way of experiencing the world.

Speaking of unique, here is another listing idea that frees you to acknowledge your way of seeing things. I call this idea "Sometimes" and I learned it from a friend, a poet who teaches high school, when he read one of my poems.

Sometimes When I Kiss You

I see blue flowers,
and sometimes a young girl
in party dress, hair
fastened with roses.

You ask if she is picking
the flowers. The flowers
are wild and I never see
what she does with her hands.

My friend told me that he would assign his students to write lists of "sometimes." I realized that by putting the word "sometimes" in front of thoughts or actions, people are freed from the pressure of feeling they have to decide if their thoughts are worthy of "always." These lines are just sometimes thoughts, even if the sometimes means only the very moment the writer is writing the thoughts.

Do a list of sometimes thoughts. Try to fill a page.

> Sometimes when the phone rings I think it is
> the President inviting me out to dinner.
> Sometimes when I want to eat cookies
> I try to stop myself.
> Sometimes when I want to eat cookies
> I just go ahead and do it.
> Sometimes when I want to eat cookies
> I offer them to someone else.
> Sometimes at dusk I think of when my children
> were in grade school and this was the busy time
> of day with dinner, homework, gymnastics lessons,
> friends staying over, trumpets and piano practicing.

THE FIVE SENSES

It may seem kindergarten-simple to write what we see, hear, taste, touch and smell, but most of us need to find our way back to that direct communication between our bodies and our environment. First, we'll discuss what has distanced us from our ability to use and report our sense experience, and then we'll discuss ways of retrieving that ability.

What We Have to Overcome

We are flooded daily with communication that is abstract, stereo-typical, sentimental and/or imprecise.

Academic and work-report writing stress generalities and abstraction to dissociate brain work from heart work. For example, here is an excerpt from an article by UCLA professor Richard Lanham in the November 1996 American Way Magazine:

> Rhetoric, for most of its 2,500-year history, was the name
> for how the Western world taught its children to speak
> and write, and to think about speaking and writing. We

might think of it as teaching "the art of expression," or more grandly, "the means of conscious life." Nowadays, we call it "communication," and its importance is, I think, universally acknowledged.

These words require only the brain to work, not the five senses. Many of us were taught to write this way. We feel self-conscious or wrong if we use personal examples or the names of things in our personal lives. We sometimes have a hard time trusting that heart thoughts, in the form of the feelings we get from images and rhythms, are valid and of interest.

Greeting card verse tries to fill the gap by alluding to feelings in a general and abstract way. The card manufacturers presume to universalize feelings to sell cards in volume. For example, here's something similar to the beginning of a verse from a card for a newly-wed couple:

The miracle of marriage
starts with a festival
Where two people
promise themselves to each other
come what may

"Miracle," "festival," "promise" and "to each other" are from the lexicon of words society approves of concerning commitment and union. "Come what may" is a catchall phrase for life and its events. And "Where two people" indicates only the obvious. There is no surprise or refreshed experience here, just words that indicate there is reason for joy and celebration but bring none of the experience of such times. There is a difference between a landscape of words and a lexicon of words. A landscape, like the one William Matthews created in his poem "Bedtime," has a terrain, a body. We must use our senses to participate. A lexicon is a list of items inside a category. We use our brain to identify the category.

Some greeting card verses intended to inspire indicate they are meant to be personalized by their titles, for example, "To Mother" or "To Grandmother." They go on in short lines with the words we have learned are appropriate to show closeness, respect and gratitude.

Mother,
you were with me yesterday
when I was growing up
with friends and family.
You shared my laughing and my cries.

"Yesterday," "friends," "family," "laughing" and "cries" are
from the lexicon of officially sanctioned words about growing up.
All we experience in reading these words is a sense that we should
honor our mothers by telling them this.

Compare these lines by Stanley Plumly in his poem "Say Summer/
For My Mother":

I could give it back to you, perhaps in a season,
say summer. I could give you leaf back, green
grass, sky full of rain, root
that won't dig deeper, the names called out
just before sundown: *Linda back, Susy back,*
Carolyn. I could give you back supper
on the porch or the room without a breath
of fresh air, back the little tears in the heat,
the hot sleep on the kitchen floor,
back the talk in the great dark,
the voices low on the lawn
so the children can't hear,
say summer, say father, say mother:
Ruth and *Mary* and *Esther*, names in a book,
names I remember—I could give back this name,
and back the breath to say it with—
we all know we'll die of our children—
back the tree bent over the water,
back the sun burning down,
back the witness back each morning.

Here the sounds and rhythms of the poem lull the listener as
lullabies lull children. The images of "leaf" and "green grass" and
"sky full of rain" and "root that won't dig deeper" are a mixed bag
of life, tangible particulars that represent so much of childhood. In
the "names called out just before sundown," we hear many mothers
calling to their children who have strayed into neighborhoods and

fields in the summer light. "I could give back this name, / and back
the breath to say it with—/ we all know we'll die of our children."
How much these three lines evoke about the existential guilt of
children over the debt they owe their parents. How can the general
words "yesterdays" and "tears" ever accomplish that?

Notice in the following cardlike verse how we are on line five
before we get any new information, which is only that the writer
feels safer somehow, not anything about how the safer feeling comes
about:

> Grandmother,
> did I ever tell you
> how much you mean to me,
> how much in having a grandmother.
> I've felt protected, happier
> just knowing you are in the world,
> loving me, caring so much.

Wouldn't it be refreshing to hear a verse that actually evoked life
at Grandmother's house so we felt the safety and pleasure? Compare
these lines by Gary Soto in his poem, "Behind Grandma's House":

Behind Grandma's House

> At ten I wanted fame. I had a comb
> And two Coke bottles, a tube of Bryl-creem.
> I borrowed a dog, one with
> Mismatched eyes and a happy tongue,
> And I wanted to prove I was tough
> In the alley, kicking over trash cans,
> A dull chime of tuna cans falling.
> I hurled light bulbs like grenades
> And men teachers held their heads,
> Fingers of blood lengthening
> On the ground. I flicked rocks at cats,
> Their goofy faces spurred with foxtails.
> I kicked fences. I shooed pigeons.
> I broke a branch from a flowering peach
> And frightened ants with a stream of piss.
> I said, "Chale," "In Your Face," and "No way

Daddy-O" to an imaginary priest
Until grandma came into the alley,
Her apron flapping in a breeze,
Her hair mussed, and said, "Let me help you,"
And punched me between the eyes.

Gary Soto's grandmother made a difference to him. How he felt cared for and protected is not a mystery—there were standards and he was to get them straight! He was safe from his own vulnerability to uncomely manners and degeneration.

Current TV news and newspaper reports also generalize, abstract and universalize feeling without exploring particular experience. Reporters broadcast phrases composed of buzz words to which we are to ascribe the expected feeling: "concerned citizens," "innocent bystanders," "tragic accidents," "brutal murders" and "senseless crime." We know how they want us to feel, but I think our feelings are dampened as a consequence of these words. We have heard them before. We can categorize and file away, compartmentalize whatever incident we are hearing about. Or, we can run it over in our minds like the videotape the stations replay for at least twenty-four hours. We feel the same anxiety until some new if-it-bleeds-show-it-first sequence makes its way onto the news, but we don't usually explore our responses, feelings and perceptions.

The language eyewitnesses use is another example of a lack of "sense making." On more than one occasion, I have heard witnesses describe a gunman who opened fire in a crowd by saying, "And then the gentleman. . . ." Gentleman? A gunman gone wild against the public? Maybe the eyewitnesses think they need higher diction because they are being interviewed for TV and the word "gentleman" transmutes into their sentences about the gunman. But as viewers, we're not supposed to notice the use of this word. The reporters don't mention it. But this language imparts undeserved elevated recognition to the gunman.

A poet is not trying to evoke a disembodied brain. A poet is not trying to appeal to mere well-wishers. A poet is not interested in increasing free-floating anxiety and blotting out individual learning and insight. And while we're at it, a poet is not a talk show host standing by while people drown out each other in words that are defensive, argumentative and terribly clichéd.

A poet is searching in quiet for a learned truth, an earned wisdom or insight, some knowledge gained from a particular lived experience. To do so, poets must write what things look, sound, taste, smell and feel like to them, separate from anyone else or what society tells them to experience. These things must be evoked through the senses—the poet reexperiences them through the environment he or she has occupied or is occupying while writing. Getting this right takes practice in our culture where we are also constantly force-fed the speech of mass marketing.

Advertising jingles direct our associations (reaching out and touching = phone calling; just doing it = athletic shoes; being number two = car rentals). Desires to consume are ignited by advertisers who study trends and demographics. In the mass-market approach, sellers count on us wanting to look unique by looking the same as everyone else. Poetry is just the opposite. It demands that we experience the world as we do, not as we would want to or as someone else would have us do it.

Advertising, news coverage, greeting cards, television talk shows and much academic and popular writing swarm around our ears and collude to thin and water down our experience, to drown out personal "intelligenciated sense" and "felt thought."

TOOLS FOR "MAKING SENSE"

Following are some exercises to help you refresh your experience by thinking in images that appeal to the five senses.

Sight

This is the sense we probably rely on most in this culture. Don't be surprised if you are more drawn to using images of sight than any other, but be sure to develop the other four as well. In the meantime, try these exercises. They ask you to use sight words without using adjectives, the words that qualify nouns. For instance, if I were describing the long, princess-style white telephone sitting on my desk, in order not to use adjectives like I just did, I could say the telephone has the shape of a tongue. If I were describing a woman in a flowered (adjective) dress, I could say that the fabric of her dress bore irises and daffodils. If I were describing my own hands, I might say they rest on my computer's keyboard the color of clams outside of their shells rather than saying they are white or clam-colored. Forcing yourself to structure your wording to avoid adjectives helps you evoke experience in a way that it can be relived.

- Show in words, without using adjectives, a person you see in a photograph.
- Show in words, without using adjectives, who you see in the mirror when you look into it.
- Show in words, without using adjectives, the food on your cupboard shelves.
- Show in words, without using adjectives, the furniture in the room where you are sitting.

Sound

We are inundated with sound—man-made and natural, delightful and annoying, jarring and ignored. See if you can get the sounds of your life into words. Devices such as onomatopoeia and alliteration can help.

Onomatopoeia is the name for the formation or use of words that imitate the sound named: buzz, hum, bumpity-bump, clump. Alliteration is the occurence of consecutive words starting with the same sound: Peter picked a peck of pickled peppers, lonely Lulu. Although the alliterative phrases don't report sound as onomatopoeia does, they do increase the sense of sound in your writing.

Write descriptions using onomatopoeia or alliteration to describe at least three of the places below. Make sure you actually visit or remember in detail a specific place for each category you choose.

- A freeway you can stand near
- A Laundromat you can go inside of
- A kitchen you are in
- A dentist's chair you've visited
- A bus stop where you wait
- A park you walk in

Before you start to describe the place you are remembering, write a detailed title, for example, Overhearing Interstate 5 from Corliss Avenue in Seattle; Sitting in Dr. Harold Berlin's Dental Chair, Circa 1956.

Smell

How something smells creates an immediate response inside of us. Smells lure and repel us. They arouse our appetites and sexual desires. They take us back to our childhoods and feelings of safety or danger. They are associated with partings, unions, arrivals, separations and abandonments. See if you can describe the following by imagining scenes and then telling about the smells in those surroundings. For instance, if I wanted to describe my hesitation about weeding my garden, I could say my hesitation smelled like sulfur in a New Jersey swamp overpowering the scents of rosemary, sage and thyme.

- Imagine your father, mother, grandparent's, teacher's or friend's anger. How does it smell?
- Imagine when you actually realized you knew how to do a particular thing or when you first demonstrated a new skill. How did that smell?
- Imagine a time you were lost. How did that smell?
- Imagine being in a room where you read a book you loved. How did those moments smell?
- Remember an altercation or time of fear you had in a house, neighborhood place, classroom, caféteria, hallway, dormitory or locker room. How did that time smell?

Taste

What do things taste like? What things in your writing have tastes?

- Name six things you can see right now that have a taste. Is it a sweet taste, a bitter taste, a sour taste, an acid taste, a clean taste, a minty taste? If you are not in a dining room, kitchen, campsite or café, the things you see might not be edible, but they could have a taste. Outside my window I see sour-tasting salmon berries. In my trash can is yesterday's yogurt container with streaks of the sweet chocolate yogurt left on it. The ink in my printer cartridge would taste bitter. The natural citrus room freshener I bought that is delightful to smell, might taste acidic.

- It is important that you wake your senses up. What is the taste of hate in your mouth? It might be burnt roast, but it might be the artificial lemon flavor that covers the chemical taste of mouthwash. What do you perceive as the taste of hate? Of love? Of laughter? Of ignorance? Of cowardice? Of humiliation? To find a flavor, think of a time you experienced each emotion. What was in the experience that might have had a taste and seems fitting to use as the flavor of that experience?

Touch

This may be the sense poets use second only to sight. To write well, we must actually relive our experience. One way we offer ourselves this reliving is by responding with our nerve endings.

• List as many touch words as you can—soft, hard, rough, smooth, irregular, bumpy, flat, round, curved, fuzzy, squishy, solid, firm, watery, cold, hot, dry, wet, frozen. I'm sure you can come up with ten to twenty more.

• Try for at least five more. Think of things you touch and how they feel anywhere on your skin. How does a pear feel to your tongue or fingers? How does an eyeliner brush feel to your eyelid? A razor to your cheek? How does a tongue feel on your tongue? How does the upholstery in your car feel on your leg when you are wearing shorts? How does sunlight feel on your arm while you are driving?

• For the phrases below, think of a particular person or object in your life and apply touch images to them:

> The skin of a child busy in play
> Your bed sheets when you crawl between them
> Your toothbrush in your mouth
> Hand lotion in your palm, along your arm or on your back
> An overripe vegetable or fruit
> The seat of the chair you are sitting in

METAPHOR AND SIMILE

Poets are always associating one thing with another in order to reawaken the senses. When they do this using "like" or "as," they are technically making similes. When they skip the "like" or "as" and just say something is something else, for example, (the gray sky is a dirty handkerchief), they are using metaphors. It doesn't matter which is which when you are writing, just that you reexperience what you are writing by using this form of associative thinking.

A warning, however: We have all heard too many times that love is like a red, red rose or someone is as hungry as a horse. They are called "tired metaphors" or clichés. In overly used comparisons, we no longer see a picture in the words or feel the experience anew. The phrases have become the same as editorializing words, conveying how to feel about the experience but not the experience itself. They don't do any work for the poet because they go straight to the head, bypassing the senses. Here are some more clichés: your eyes are windows to your soul, this thought hit me over the head, reach out and touch someone. Keep a list of clichés you find yourself or others using so you can catch yourself and find more surprising ways of expressing yourself.

A poem that I wrote after my daughter had a bad fall at age four (she recovered and grew up just fine) relies heavily on simile and metaphor:

Folding

You are folding the clothes of a child
and thinking about this afternoon and the month after next
when the ghost of your husband carries the ghost of your girl,
"She's fallen 6 feet from the porch rail to the sidewalk,"
and the child sleeps in his arms breath shallow as at birth.

Touch her skin and you feel it collapse like a parachute.
Watch her eyes flicker open, they are murky, do not reflect
even the clouds up there waiting to come together,
and now the future waits,
all of you suddenly pinched behind the neck.

In the next minutes she will respond to her name.
You can see in her waking
there *are* clouds in her eyes
and you remember her saying this morning
her friends believed god lived in the sky
but she knew she would have seen him up there
riding the clouds and anyway she'd heard on television
that god had a purple head.

The hours in intensive care you will watch
clouds sheet the sky like hospital linen
and hear the chirp of heart monitors like crickets
out of place in the night.

This night you are a stage mother pushing
your child to perform for neurologists and nurses
in the reciting of names, her own, her brother's, her dog's,
in the telling of how many fingers
and the matching of her finger to theirs.

After this only waiting is left.
Hours unfold out of themselves like a telescope
and you watch the sky turn the lightest shade of purple.

Then you pray to her god and to all
the grape popsicles in the freezer, to her purple crayon,
to the foxglove and alyssum in the yard,
to all purple things that they may keep their color,
retrieve it from her bruised forehead, ear, stem of her brain.

I was in a state of shock when I wrote this poem. My daughter
was in the critical care unit and we were waiting for signs that her
severe concussion was not going to leave her brain damaged. I could
hardly feel. But by using sense images and constructing metaphors
and similes with those images in the poem, I brought the experience
of that day into my being. I felt it.

Sometimes it takes some doing to get the mind to loosen up and
create metaphors and similes. I learned an easy exercise for practicing this way of thinking from David Greenberg in his book, *Teaching
Poetry to Children*. All you do is imagine one thing is like another
thing: a rainbow is like a tiara, straps on my Birkenstock sandals are
like two highway overpasses, chickweed in the garden is like my
son's curly hair, my son's kayak is like a pea pod, my daughter's
fingers on the piano keys are like the swirls of white water over
rocks.

To grease the wheels of your own metaphor-making, do three
things:

1. Collect metaphors and similes that strike you from your reading. Keep a notebook of them. Novelists as well as poets use them
a lot.

2. Challenge yourself to play the like game several times a week.
Make up five beginnings in the morning or five at the start of a
week, and fill in the endings by evening or the end of the week.
Play with your kids, friends or partner. If they don't want to do
the endings, let them supply the beginnings. Let them know what
you wrote for each. Keep lists of what you've done. Read the lists
of metaphors from time to time. Which ones make your hair raise
a little or give you a shudder of delight or make you sigh with
poignancy? They're the ones getting right through to your senses

without needing to go through the brain. They are supplying direct experience and are a delight.

    3. Do the "sometimes" exercise and incorporate "likes" into it:

> Sometimes when I walk home in fall, I think I am a queen
> and all the leaves on the ground are my subjects.
> Sometimes when I open the refrigerator after a busy week, I think
>   I am a rat in a compost heap.
> Sometimes when I pick up the phone and it is you, I feel like I'm
>   a ping pong ball slammed hard over the net.
> Sometimes when I fall asleep, I float in dark green water.

BANTU

Recently I was standing on a hillside I had looked at years ago from a window at a writers conference. At that conference, I learned a useful exercise from my teacher Robert Hass, who went on to become the United States poet laureate. At the time, he was studying various culture's poetry using a book called *Technicians of the Sacred*. In Africa, he taught us, a tribe called the Bantu have an oral poetic tradition they exercise while working. One person says a line and, in the rhythm of the work, another answers with an association that shows the likeness between two objects or perceptions. "An elephant's tusk cracking," could get the response, "The voice of an angry man." That day, I looked at the hillside, saw wind in the grass and wrote, "Wind through the grass," and answered with the line, "I have the feeling you have written." Here are two-line bantus that students of mine have written in response to this exercise:

> Wire hangers on a bar in the closet
> Wild geese walking by a lake

> Children in a circle on the floor
> The beaded necklace

> Lizard rustles the jasmine leaves
> Father turning pages of *The Sunday NY Times*

> My mother when she comes home from work
> A vase cracking

The smell of fresh bread in a bakery
Clothes just out of the dryer

The full moon at midnight
China dinner plate in a dark kitchen

Write your own bantus, as many as you can. Try to evoke experiences of sound, taste and smell as well as touch and sight. This exercise is very much like metaphor and simile, but you are free of the need to make the images grammatically correct and the results can be haunting.

◆ ◆ ◆

Now that you have had some practice using the tools of poetry, let's move on to some strategies for allowing poems to arrive—to disturb that cactus and make the needle jump.

CHAPTER FIVE

Beginning to Create Poems

*If an exercise leaves you better equipped to write the next poem,
then it has done its job.*
       —from the introduction to
       The Practice of Poetry,
       edited by Robin Behn and Chase Twichell

In his book, *The Heart Aroused*, David Whyte refers to "the heaven of firsthand experience" which he describes as possible when we have nowhere to go and need nothing to feel complete. For poets, this happens in the work of creating a poem. But how can this happen when we need the words to feel complete, when we want more than anything to have the poem finished? This is a wonderful paradox and delight of writing poetry: Using words, we actually get to a place where the words bring us experience and we are completely at home there, and the words that compose the experience are in charge. We don't dwell on a need to say something smart; we're not even aware of working to finish the poem. Getting to the end is just part of the experience we are having with the words. Most poets report feeling the words bringing wisdom and speaking it through them rather than the poets speaking through the words. In his *Memoirs*, Pablo Neruda describes his experience of being with words:

> I catch them in midflight, as they buzz past, I trap them, clean them, peel them, I set myself in front of the dish, they have a crystalline texture to me, vibrant, ivory, vegetable, oily, like fruit, like algae, like agates, like olives. . . ."

How can we step into that heaven? Luckily, just by playing with words. Following are some prompts and strategies for playing in a way that will create poems.

SOME PROMPTS FOR CREATING POEMS
Nobody Knows

Practice the list technique from the last chapter combined with a twist. So many times we list, over and over again, both in our inner dialogue and with others, what we have said, seen and done. "I said this and then I did so and so and then I saw him look such and such." I want you to enter the realm of silence that many say is at the center of poetry by listing what you never said, what you never saw and what you never did before you list what you did say, what you did see and what you did do. The poem lies in the juxtaposition of the two scenarios.

Begin by using a technique called clustering that was introduced by Gabriele Rico in her book, *Writing the Natural Way*. In the center of a blank piece of paper, write the words "sad situation" or "happy situation" or "mysterious situation" or "irritating situation." Do this exercise four times, one for each phrase. Circle the phrase you have written in the center of your page. Now freely associate times that apply to the phrase. Each time you think of one, draw a line from the center circled phrase. Write a short description of the situation you are thinking of at the end of the line and then circle that. If you think of some details, including what you did or didn't say, see or do, write those at the end of lines radiating out from the circles around the situations you are thinking about. Then circle each of these details. If you think of another situation stemming from the central phrase, repeat this process. Circling helps you get into the groove of associating and recalling, of being ready for a surprise.

On page 58 is a cluster that I have done around "irritating situations."

Go ahead and do clusters for the situation phrases above. You should have a feeling about one of the situations that you want to write about it. Begin writing about it by giving it a title, for example, "When My Husband Spoke Each Night for a Week About a Friend's Divorce" came to me from my details in the "irritating situation" scenario.

Next, write sentences that finish these starts:

I didn't say _____

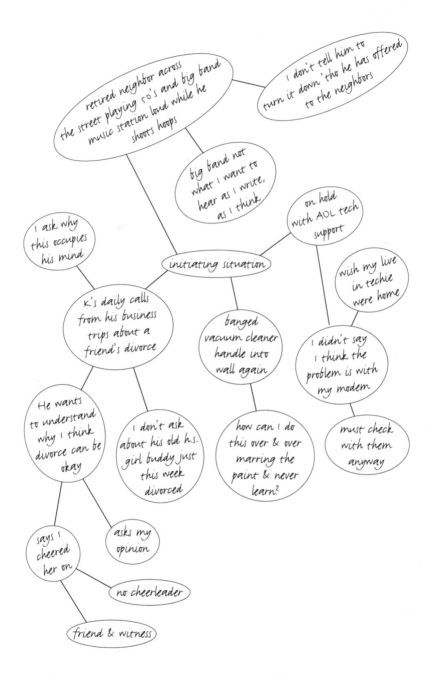

retired neighbor across the street playing 50's and big band music station loud while he shoots hoops

I don't tell him to turn it down 'tho he has offered to the neighbors

big band not what I want to hear as I write, as I think

on hold with AOL tech support

I ask why this occupies his mind

initiating situation

wish my live in techie were home

K's daily calls from his business trips about a friend's divorce

banged vacuum cleaner handle into wall again

I didn't say I think the problem is with my modem

He wants to understand why I think divorce can be okay

I don't ask about his old h.s. girl buddy just this week divorced

how can I do this over & over marring the paint & never learn?

must check with them anyway

says I cheered her on

asks my opinion

no cheerleader

friend & witness

I didn't see _____
I didn't_____ (action) _____

Leave a break of white space and begin again:
I said _____
I saw _____
I _____ (action) _____

What you have done is create two stanzas—that is the word we use in poetry writing to mean units of thought. In the free verse most contemporary poets use, which is not routinely metered, rhymed or qualified in terms of number of lines, a poem can have one or more stanzas. Stanzas can be of equal or varying length. What they accomplish is to work against that silence. The evenness between each stanza here is supplied by the parallelism of said, saw, did. The reason for making two stanzas is to speak to the contrast (or to let the contrast speak) between what was visible and what was invisible. In that contrast, true experience is evoked.

Here is an example of my work from the prompts and title. After clustering on the subject of irritating situations and thinking of some of the details of this particular situation, I realized I had nagging questions: Why was K talking about a friend's divorce so much? Why did it annoy me that he was?

> *When My Husband Spoke Long Distance*
> *Each Night for a Week About a Friend's Divorce*

I didn't say, "Are you questioning our marriage
because your best girl buddy from high school's
divorce is final this week?"
I didn't see his fingers move like an ice flow
cooling the warm ocean of his auburn hair.
I didn't close my eyes.

I said I saw the deer had visited our yard twice that day,
a buck, a doe, two spotted fawns.
I saw through my window the wild flower patch
where they had nibbled from the green, green leaves.
I went outside to count the chewed off stems,
to see which flowers had appealed to them.

Check your work. Because we are trying to evoke rather than tell experience, it is necessary for the details and images to appeal to the senses. Did you use words that appeal to several of the five senses? Were you using specific details from the situation's environment? For instance, if you didn't see the clock, did you tell where it hung on the wall, next to what? "I didn't see the clock that hung on the wall next to the open door." Did you use metaphor or simile? "I didn't see the clock round as a French beret that hung on the wall next to the open door." Did you include snippets of dialogue so the dialogue could speak for itself, or did you merely summarize the dialogue and distance the experience of it? "I didn't say, 'Your socks have holes at the toes, more fragile than buttonholes. Your shirts lie crumpled on the floor, the jigsaw puzzle of your days.' " A mistake would be to say, "I didn't tell him about the holes in his socks and the way he left his shirts crumpled on the floor."

Review your responses to the exercise and rewrite them if you want. Strive to use the tools from chapter four.

This Is I

When you move through your days, you may forget to check inside of yourself to see how you are doing and what you are feeling. This next exercise forces you to pay attention to yourself.

In the evening, think back over your day. What did you do? Shop for something? Get stuck in traffic? Hit golf balls at a driving range with a friend or your child? Wait in line at the post office? Sit on a bus? Attend a meeting? Write a memo? Hold for someone on the phone? Get interrupted by call waiting? Face a pile of paper or give instructions to people? Get admonished by someone? Admonish someone? Fix lunch or dinner? Order lunch or dinner? Get coffee? Bath children? Write checks? Read the paper? Watch the news?

Write down things that you did or situations you found yourself in. Be precise and detailed. You can use the clustering technique to conjure this material.

An example of such a cluster can be seen on page 61.

When you are ready to write, start with the title, "This Is I." Begin as many lines as you like with the words, "This is I who. . . ." Fill in the actions and situations of your day. Use remembered bits of dialogue. After you have used lines to show what you did or where you were in the outer life, start filling in feelings and thoughts. Make

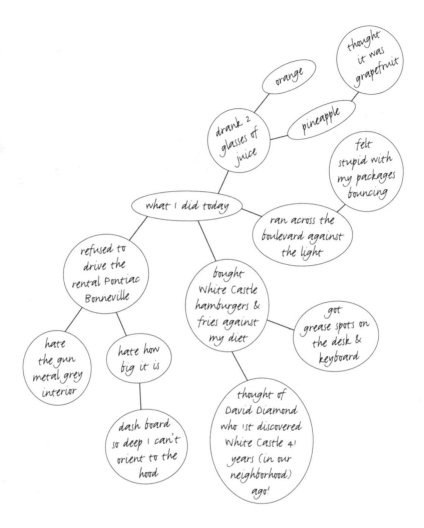

them precise and detailed. Use sensory words. Use metaphor. Here is an example drawn from the cluster I did above:

This Is I

This is I who ran across the broad Birmingham, MI
boulevard against the light, the altered slacks
I'd just picked up streaming over my shoulder
in their plastic cover, like a river over
my back pack.

This is I who ordered *two hamburgers*
with everything and a small fries from the tiny
White Castle which reminds me
of my NJ childhood in a new house
next to the part of Bardy Farms not yet
sold off to those developers.

This is I who bought some flowered stationery
in a florist's shop and heard her apologize
for the delay in taking my money—too much
happening and staff not in. It was I who said
That's okay. I have plenty of time today.

It was I who heard her when she said
I should hire you for the day.
You have plenty of time and I don't.

It was I who answered *I wouldn't be*
any good at what you'd need me to do.
You'd be surprised, she said. *One does*
flower arranging naturally.

It was I who remembered picking wild
flowers, putting them in a mason jar,
watching a lady bug crawl across the counter.

It was I who heard the florist ask
Can you use peach? The silk rose wreathes
are for all year. You just add something to them.
A beautiful bow will do, plaid for French
country. White for formality. They're fifty
percent off now. Not everyone can use them.

Tonight

In writing, starting where you are is very helpful. Begin this exercise early or late evening. Look at what you can see from where you write—the sky, a lake, the ocean, a garden, a lawn, the dining room table, the breakfast nook, the countertops, the front door, the steering column of your car, the soapy circles of glass in the front of washing machines at the Laundromat.

Cluster or list at least five reasons you are looking at this place. For the steering wheel I might write: because I am driving home from work, because I hold it in my two hands, because I must turn left, because I must turn right, because I must go straight. Look at your cluster or list and think about your reasons. Next, write a title beginning with the word "tonight" that might allow for many of the reasons to be in one poem. For the example I have been using, "Tonight I Drive My Heart Home From Work" occurs to me.

Tonight I Drive My Heart Home From Work

Suddenly I notice the steering wheel,
its lanyard-laced leather cover,
now smooth as porcelain in my hands.

Perhaps these past five years a rougher
leather held my hands in its grip,
turning left, turning right.
Tonight I see a new surface
so smooth I fear my grip
could shatter it.

When I Saw You

How many times have you suddenly been overcome with strong feelings just watching someone do something? In writing poetry, we take time to note these feelings. Begin a cluster or list of people you remember watching when these deep feelings occurred. You might want to stay away from anger, which usually covers up a more basic feeling such as sorrow or fear. And think small. Instead of choosing something large like the time your husband surprised you with a new car, try the time your son came home from the pet shop with his first goldfish. What did his clothes look like? The bag in his hand? His hair and his eyes? Did he know the fish needed to stay in the bag in the sink for awhile while the water in the fish bowl became room temperature?

Here is a list of common places and actions in which you may have observed someone and had these deep feelings:
- When I saw you put your hands in the soapy dish water
- When I saw your peanut butter cheek
- When I saw the ring that pierces your brown eyebrow

- When I saw you assembling the gas grill
- When I saw you raking leaves
- When I saw the unmatched socks you were wearing
- When I saw the elevator doors close in front of you
- When I saw you lie down at the edge of the bed

Use one of these or make up your own situation. If you want to get some ideas from clustering, do a cluster around the phrase "When I saw" and think of people you know in places they commonly are or doing things they commonly do. Another way is to think of someone you love or miss and cluster around the following phrase, inserting their name: "I see Jason doing _____."

Let the title be a "When I saw you . . ." phrase. Then write lines that detail what you saw. You can go on to what you heard or thought, remembered or smelled, touched or tasted. Remember the ease with which you can make lists, the value of words that appeal to the senses and metaphor, and the poetic value of juxtaposing outward images with inward images.

Do this one on your own. We'll see some samples of student responses in the next chapters.

THREE DAYS AND THREE NIGHTS

In *The Heart Aroused*, David Whyte says that "the mythic code for 'a very long time' is usually 'three days and three nights.'" He says many scholars think the "three days and three nights" refer to the three nights each month when the moon is not in the sky.

Let's combine this notion of a dark stretch of time with another one.

I read a column in the University of California at Berkeley's student paper about ten years ago. A chemistry student from the Middle East was relating how, new to America, he kept noticing people outside his classes and lab talking about "the solution to the problem." He imagined a chemical solution in which a problem dissolved—not to be solved, but to come out of the solution somehow altered. He was musing about how this might be more like what really happens in life.

Write a poem called "Three Days and Three Nights." Write at the same time each day or night for three sessions. Or write at three randomly scattered times over that same period. Begin each section with the date or the time of day or night you are writing.

Before you begin, though, cluster on the phrase "a problem." Think of the problems in your life, who else is involved, what the elements involved are and why they are not solvable right now. Choose one problem to concentrate on. When you write each time, be sure to include details of your day or night and of the problem. You don't have to be conscious of the details of the day that relate to the problem, just ones that seem right to include. See what happens each time you write about the problem without striving to solve the problem. "Three Days and Three Nights" will be the solution into which you drop your problem. See what happens after that "very long time."

Again, do this on your own. Later, we will work with an example from a student's work.

DREAMS

Keep a dream journal because dreams supply vivid images. The more you write down your dreams, the more you remember.

See if you can make a poem from a dream. You can be very direct. Start the first stanza, "In my dream. . . ."

After you have retold your dream using the images you can remember, start a second stanza one of these ways:

I tell you this and you . . .

I would tell you this, but . . .

I almost forget my dream, _____
(any action such as eating, listening or running)

Use details and images from your real life or the life of the "you" you select here. Again, we'll work with some of the results of this strategy exercise in the following chapters.

MAIL

So many of us have voice mail and E-mail and use postal mail with its various levels of service—express, parcel post, priority, book rate, and so on. How many ways can you use these various mails to help generate poems? Here are a few of my ideas.

Voice Mail

1. Write a different greeting for every day of the week, for every month or for every season.

2. Write messages you might leave for someone on certain days such as the equinox, the full moon or the new moon.

Postcards

1. Imagine someone who thinks your daily life takes place in a choice vacation spot. Send them a series of postcard messages from your home that will help them see things this way.

2. Think of occasions that are not usually handled by postcard—asking someone to marry you, resigning a job or filing your taxes. Write a postcard poem to someone upon such an occasion. Think of exactly what is on the other side of this postcard—where you are writing from, why you chose this card.

Book Rate

When you mail printed material book rate, you are not supposed to include a personal letter or any handwritten information in the envelope. Imagine a message you might sneak into a parcel sent book rate. Would you type it and put it between the pages? Would you write it in ink on the inside cover of the book? Would you photocopy it and put the copy in the package? Why would you send someone a message book rate? Would you be hoping the message was a surprise, that the recipient would unexpectedly come across it upon opening the book or turning the pages?

Write a poem that is the message. Use a title to tell who you are writing to and where this message is.

The Missing Eighty Miles (Persona, Personification)

My husband's car's gas meter is broken. When he fills his tank, he always puts the trip odometer to zero and knows that when it reads four hundred miles, he's running on empty. One weekend, exploring the Olympic Peninsula, we were in a small town when he said, "Well, we have eighty more miles, but I may as well fill the car up now." After he paid for the gas, he said, "Well, that's four hundred more miles." I said, "Don't you mean 480?" OK, so everyone we tell this story to falls out of their chairs laughing, but it is my poetry mind at work that got me hung up like that.

Those eighty miles he said we had left lodged in my brain as their own entity and I wasn't about to give them up. Where would we be when we had driven those eighty miles? How would we be?

They had taken on a life, my life; therefore, I couldn't believe they had blended in with the next tank of gas.

Write a poem called "The Next Eighty Miles." Think of where you will drive, or be driven, your next eighty miles. Describe exactly what you see, hear, taste, touch and smell along the roads of these miles. Tell where you start and where you end, outside and in.

You might want to try your hand at a persona poem. If these miles could talk, what would they tell you? Think of the roads talking to you, or the tires of the car, or the windshield washers. Whatever you think can speak with a voice you can write.

Frank O'Hara wrote a poem called, "A True Account of Talking to the Sun at Fire Island." You might want to look it up in a collection of his work or in the poetry writing book *Sleeping on the Wing*. In the poem, the sun comes to awaken Mr. O'Hara, having something important to tell him. The poet personified the nonhuman sun. Try letting the miles have their say in your work. Again, we will check on some results of this strategy in the following chapters.

Dialogue

You already know from my examples and exercises that poems often contain direct speech. Poets hear something someone has said, or remember what they have said to someone or something, and they include these lines in their poems, sometimes repeating them more than once. In my poem "Folding" in chapter four, I report the direct speech of the husband. Often in drafting a poem, I use more dialogue than what is in the final version. Words that I or other people have spoken can help a poem come into being. A poem can even be a conversation. (You might want to look at *Meadowlands*, a recent poetry collection by award-winning poet Louise Glück, whose poems are the dialogue of a doomed couple.)

To get used to using dialogue, go to a café, store or other place where people gather. Write four sentences that you overhear. Write a poem that uses each of the four sentences. There are several ways to do this:

1. Write a title that tells where you were when you heard these words, for example, "Standing in the Checkout Line at Safeway." List the dialogue in the first lines of your poem and then evoke the situation in which they were overheard.

2. Make each line the opening of a new stanza. Write your own response to each line. This can be conversation between your own

or never-meant-to-be-spoken, meditative thoughts. When you are done, see if you can title this work in a way that draws the stanzas together, for example, "Tuesday Afternoon Meditation in Starbuck's."

3. Write a poem that incorporates each line of dialogue as if they were just lines in the poem.

You may find it useful to write more overheard sentences and then use the ones that are most lyrical, interesting or suggestive for your poem.

◆ ◆ ◆

Now that you have begun to write poems, you likely have many questions about shaping and tuning them so they can stand as strong pieces of work. In the next chapters, we'll look at what my students wrote in response to the exercises in these last two chapters. We'll look at what makes a poem a poem: its landscape; its occasion and speaker; its compression; its balance between narrative and lyric language; and its use of line, rhythm and tone.

CHAPTER SIX

Shaping Poems From Your Beginnings

When a good poet looks at an object with the eyes in his head, he sees more than merely accurately.
        —*John Holmes*
        Writing Poetry

I enjoy teaching new poets to use the tools of poetry without worrying about how what is written will end up becoming poetry. After they've played with the tools and experienced something of the poet's stance, we go back to what they wrote in response to the first tool-using exercises—the lists—and look for material they want to develop into a poem.

What is it we identify and what do I ask them for? Let's follow the beginning writing of new poet Judy Tough.

SHAPING POEMS FROM LIST EXERCISES

In doing the lists exercise, Judy was attracted to listing what was in her refrigerator and why it was there. She was not required to do great writing, just to say something about each item. Sometimes she repeated the phrases, " 'easy' was the watchword" and "my culinary arts aren't what they should be." Sometimes she phrased sentences loosely and editing would tighten them, but that was not necessary here. Judy didn't have to, and was wise not to, engage the editor part of herself in doing this exercise. Writing the lists is for generating thoughts, feelings and material without worry. Freedom from editorial restraint pays off in the beginning processes because it allows the unconscious to gather material without bowing to judgment.

You might ask, "But how does judging one phrase as repetitive and finding another way to say something keep the unconscious from working its way into the writing process?" Think of the un-conscious as very sensitive and shy. It stays away when the harder, analytical, rule-abiding conscious self takes over and goes to work.

Here is Judy's list, titled, "Refrigerator Items and Why They Are There."

1. Peach Butter. Having a fruit-bearing tree in my new garden is a novelty to me as is retirement. "This can't go to waste" was the compelling thought which led to me searching for a method of preserving this food. My culinary arts have lain dormant for nearly 3 decades while I was pursuing my career so "easy" was the watchword for a recipe! Hence, several different size jars of peach butter reside in the back of one shelf.

2. Chutney. John, the landscape artist hired to "remodel" our new garden, wanted to know if I wanted two large rhubarb plants. No, one would do, I said. But now I had rhubarb! "This can't go to waste" was the compelling thought which led to searching for a method of preserving this food. And since my culinary arts aren't what they could be, "easy " was the watchword for a recipe! Hence, several different size containers of rhubarb, plum and fig chutney reside somewhere within the refrigerator.

3. Frozen Yogurt. In the refrigerator? I hear you say. Well, yes. Since easy was the watchword and my culinary arts aren't what they should be, sooner or later there was bound to be a misjudgment, a blunder, a botch. Peaches from the tree and raspberries from the garden patch were combined (under guidance of a recipe) with other ingredients to make the heralded low-fat dessert. Alas, once frozen it was so hard we couldn't chip it from the plastic bowl! So it sits on the front of the refrigerator shelf to remind us to eat the soupy, but tasty, stuff quickly.

4. Talking Rain Mineral Water. I became a fan of flavored and non-flavored waters several years ago. When we joined the discount house Costco after moving here, I was delighted to find cases of this mineral water available for a very good price. And I am delighted with the name as I am with the tastes.

5. Bean Soup. One of our favorite soups that gets better tasting the longer it sits in the fridge. Now that the weather is sometimes nippy, it seemed a good dish to keep on hand for quick meals.

6. Chopped Green Chilies. I got a can of them for a recipe and it seemed a waste to throw the rest out, so I keep thinking that maybe I'll think of some way to use up the rest of them.

7. Black Bean Sauce. This jarred Chinese sauce is a favorite for putting on chicken breasts and grilling.

FINDING A POEM'S OCCASION

We talked about the entries and what Judy wrote about them because we wanted an answer to the question, "Upon what occasion would the writer be prompted to speak about the item or items listed?" The occasion may have something to do with the "why" it is in the refrigerator, or it may have to do with other feeling associations. Translating the items on the list into occasions can result in titles addressing certain moments such as "Shopping for Talking Rain" and "Using Up Green Chilies." Only the writer really knows the meaningful occasion and can have the "Aha, that resonates for me. I feel compelled to explore this" experience.

To shape poems from your beginnings, it helps to discuss the results of your exercises with a trusted reader. If you rely on yourself without showing the work to anyone else, try to talk to yourself about your work as if you were not the one who wrote it. The talk, whether between you and a trusted reader or between you and yourself, must only be aimed at facilitating that "aha" moment. This is done by having the responder/listener give the writer a response in three steps: repeat the words and phrases that stick, tell what feelings seem to be in the work so far and tell what keeps the listener from fully engaging in the experience and feeling. That last step means pointing out where more information is wanted, or where changes in tone engender unwanted, distracting feelings.

When Judy and I looked at her list, I told her what images and phrases caught my attention. I said, in Peach Butter, it was the garden being as novel as retirement and the image of the several-sized jars. I found myself wanting to hear from this "new canner," and proposed that this could be a title and an occasion upon which to speak. Under Chutney, I was attracted to the names of the fruit and again the "several different-size containers." Could she be more specific about these containers? What were they exactly? It turned out she had been envisioning the same jars as the ones she used to can the peaches, her mother's several-sized jar collection, which she'd just stored in her basement. It was beginning to sound like this was a deeper occasion for Judy than just canning for the first time. It was the occasion of filling her mother's empty jars.

I proposed the title "Filling My Mother's Jars With Peach Butter and Rhubarb Chutney," and Judy went on to write more, concentrating on using detail and imagery:

> In the garden of our new house is a tree of sun-ripened peaches and a large plant of ruby red rhubarb. These are novelties to me, as is retirement, and after three decades of a time-demanding career my culinary skills are ripe for cultivation.
>
> Enthusiastically, I pore through cookbooks, researching possibilities. Then, and only then, do I realize that I no longer have the stash of odd glass jars that resided on the top shelf of a kitchen cabinet in my old house 2,600 miles away. What will I put this bubbling sweet smelling stuff into? How will I store it until its needed? And I remember that I have, in the basement, boxes of mementos my mother couldn't part with when she moved into an assisted living facility that is one third the living space of her old house. She didn't have room for her jars nor did she have the need to use them. No longer will bubbly sweet things be cooked in her kitchen, you see, meals are provided for the residents. As I fill my mother's jars, I wonder what my mother will have in her new garden. Will it be ruby red roses and sun-laden memories, sweet produce cultivated by a life long lived? And will I be able to fill my mother's jars with patience, understanding and love should the crop be bitter berries and silence?

Now there were so many more details and images to work with. There was a nice complexity, too, in the twining of the speaker's retirement with her new home and garden and her mother's move. The speaker's new home has fruit trees and plants and her mother's jars; the mother's new home is not large enough for the past, so the speaker must condense the past, boil the sweet essence from it and fill her mother's jars, all the while wondering if she will be up to the task of loving her aging mother. There is a major life shift here and the story can be told in the act of filling the jars.

USING WORDS THAT SHOW INSTEAD OF TELL

But instead of thinking theme and importance, the writer must think craft and images, sounds and word choices. The writer can push a paragraph like Judy's toward poetry by looking for the places that the eyes, ears and heart are most interested in and the places that block that interest. My responses went like this:

I remember vividly the sun-ripened peaches, the ruby red rhubarb, the culinary skills ripe for cultivation, the cookbooks, odd glass jars, boxes in the basement and bitter berries.

I felt the poignancy of the speaker's reflection about this time in her life. Just as she is free to enjoy time and nature, her mother is being restricted in what she can outwardly do.

What is in the way of my moving with the speaker into her moment of insight and feeling this particular life experience? Well, certain word choices put up barriers.

The word "enthusiastically," for instance, takes me away from the speaker and her situation. I see the speaker clearly in "I pore through cookbooks." The word "pore" imparts a tone and I get to feel it. The word "enthusiastically" tells me how to feel, but doesn't let me actually feel as a consequence of what comes in through my senses. Enthusiastically is what we call an *editorial* word. It tells readers how they should interpret what the writer experienced rather than allowing them to experience the moment themselves. "Researching possibilities" is a *summarizing* phrase; it stands for all the recipes. A summarizing word makes me aware that someone is writing this when what I want is to be submerged in the moment itself, unaware of the writer and aware only of the moment. "Pore through cookbooks" implies searching for possibilities and is immediate by itself. "Then and only then" is another phrase that makes me feel, in its insistence, that there is a writer writing this and thus removes me from the immediate experience. I am with the "then" and I don't need to think of other "thens." "I remember that I have" seems to slow things up; "In the basement there are boxes" seems quicker, more alive in the moment. Next, "of mementos" slows me down again. "Mementos" is a categorizing, summarizing word. What exactly is in the boxes?

My recommendation was to remove some words, look for possible line breaks and then retype her work so we could see the poem it was becoming. Here is what it looked like in the next stage:

Filling My Mother's Jars With Peach Butter and
Rhubarb Chutney

In the garden of my new house is a tree of sun ripened peaches
and a large plant of ruby red rhubarb. These are novelties to me,
   as is retirement,
and after three decades of time-demanding career
my culinary skills are ripe for cultivation. I pore through cookbooks
then realize I no longer have the stash of odd glass jars from the
   top shelf
of my kitchen cabinet in my old house 2600 miles away.

Into what will I put this bubbling sweet smelling stuff? I remember
in my basement are boxes of things my mother couldn't part with
   when she moved
here six weeks ago into assisted living. Each object wrapped in
   sighs:
antiques, afghans, pillows, pictures, jewelry and jars,
items that did not fit as they had in her house 3500 miles away.

As I fill my mother's jars, I worry. Melancholy and sorrow furrow
   her brow,
sighs pepper her conversations: was it wise to bring her here?
I wonder, what will mother find in her new garden? Ruby red roses
and sun-laden memories; sweet produce cultivated by a life long
   lived?
And will I be able to fill my mother's jars with patience,
   understanding and love
should her crop be bitter berries and silence?

MAKING LINE AND STANZA BREAKS

Using line breaks to incorporate the feeling of the poem-to-be gave
Judy a boost as she continued to look for the shape of the final poem.
In this first step with line breaks, the poem-to-be was lifted from
the prosy roots of the exercise. Now Judy had to think about what
the lines in a poem demand. Then she could sculpt the work further.

First, the lines of a poem must not only interest the eye, they
must serve motivational and emotional functions as well. Most of
the time, the lines should end before readers feel informationally
complete so they quickly return to the next word. But a line must

also contain enough of a unit of feeling or information that the heart of the reader feels full before it goes on. One way of achieving these demands is to place substantial words at the beginnings and ends of lines and to watch for unintentional repetitions of words right underneath each other. Of the six lines, in Judy's first stanza above, all start with small words and two in a row start with the same word, "and." In the second stanza, the first three lines all have small word openings, and the third stanza again has two lines in a row starting with the word "and."

Before we rearrange the line endings and beginnings, however, let's look for phrases and words that may be unnecessary because the imagery already relays the idea or feeling. Then we will be making lines with the words that do the most work. "These are novelties to me, as is retirement" seems to restate what is already inherent in the information of a new house, a thirty-year career ended and culinary skills ripe for cultivation. In fact, the phrase "culinary skills ripe for cultivation" actually conveys that idea with the most feeling because of the repeated "c" sound and the inherent association of the words "cultivation" and "ripe" with the world of her fruit trees.

Next, "each object" sounds so clinical next to the list of what the objects actually are. "Melancholy and sorrow furrow her brow, sighs pepper her conversations" are words that take my attention away from the speaker and make me look at her mother, but I don't really see her mother, only a summary of what the speaker sees. What do melancholy and sorrow look like on a face? Additionally, having sighs peppering conversation seems an unfortunate verb choice here. Pepper contrasts so much with the sweet smell I got from the bubbling stuff. This contrast makes the pepper stand out because ingredients matter in this poem, which is written on the occasion of canning peach butter and rhubarb chutney. Finally, the word "items" seems unnecessary after the list of interesting specific items.

Here is Judy's poem sculpted further:

Filling My Mother's Jars With Peach Butter and
Rhubarb Chutney

In the garden of my new house is a tree
of sun-ripened peaches and a large plant of ruby
red rhubarb. After three decades of time-demanding

career, my culinary skills are ripe for cultivation.
I pore through cookbooks, then realize I don't have
the stash of odd glass jars from on top of my old
kitchen cabinets 2600 miles away. Into what
will I put this bubbling sweet smelling stuff?

Then I remember I have boxes of what my mother
couldn't part with when I moved her here six weeks ago
into assisted living: antiques, afghans, pillows,
pictures, jewelry and jars, wrapped in sighs
because they would not fit in her apartment.
I fill my mother's jars and worry. Was it wise to bring
her here? What will she find in her new garden?
Ruby red roses and sun-laden memories, sweet produce
of a life long lived? And what if my mother's crop be silence
and bitter berries? Will I be able to fill those jars
with patience, love, and understanding?

The first stanza is now eight lines instead of six. The lengthening helps the poem in two ways: It certainly looks better not to have the "ands" right underneath each other. And moving the question, "Into what will I put this bubbling sweet smelling stuff?" into the first stanza accomplishes something that merits more discussion.

NARRATIVE AND LYRIC WORK TOGETHER

Every poem's occasion is spoken through lyric and narrative values. The narrative is the story through time and the lyric is the all-at-onceness that images create as they link in the matrix of the poem. The narrative here is simple: the speaker wants to prepare chutney and jam, finds her mother's jars, fills them and realizes an emotional situation that needs filling. In this revised version of the poem, each of the three events in the narrative occurs in time order in one of the stanzas. Having a clear narrative line allows the poem to move unobstructed toward its emotional occasion. The lyric, supplied by the sweet and bitter fruit images the words "cultivation" and "ripe," and the roses and jars, works strongly inside the narrative and offers us the feeling behind the occasion.

In the final version of the poem, the ending lines are reversed from how they were earlier. The bigger abstract words—patience, love and understanding—are last and the more tangible images of bitter berries and silence are before them. Lyric works best that way. First the tangible, so the experience can be deeply felt; then move into the larger abstract words, always sparsely used. This moment of filling the jars allows the speaker and us to experience self-assessment, and we are prepared to experience it.

SOME MORE EXAMPLES AND DISCUSSION

New poet Bev Parsons also wrote a list of things that were in her refrigerator. One of the items was "champagne left over from my boyfriend's birthday party. He bought 10 bottles and we only drank 3." In a list of occasions when she wished she could have disappeared, that same party came up again: "My boyfriend's birthday party in our apartment when, in front of all of our friends, he told his ex-lover and her son that he loved them more than anyone else on earth." This seemed like an emotional occasion Bev might want to write about; perhaps the champagne would work its way into the specifics of the party. Here is the first draft of Bev's poem:

This Occasion

13 bottles of
champagne, folding chairs
a store bought cake
with your name on it
my fear
your hospitality

The chairs leaned up
against the wall
waiting for more guests

My favorite music
your apprehension about the neighbors
then everyone arrives

The cake with your
name on it
and you open the gifts

my friends are there too

Your favorite gift is
the journal from me
a brown and tan Buddha
solid on the cover

You love everyone here
you said so
it's your party

Words that attract me: 13 bottles of champagne, chairs leaned up,
my favorite music, apprehension about the neighbors, cake with his
name on it, journal with a brown and tan Buddha on the cover. The
feeling seems to be about not quite fitting in at an important celebration. The speaker's favorite music is a matter of concern for the you
whose party it is. The "chairs leaned up against the wall waiting for
more guests" seem a little apart from things, which is how the speaker
may be feeling. The store-bought cake seems hasty, perhaps not what
she would have wished to supply for the you.

What is in the way of truly experiencing the party and realizing the
emotional occasion from which she writes? The line, "my friends are
there too" takes me out of the party I am experiencing. I don't know
why new information is important because before the cake and the
opening of gifts, I was told all the guests had arrived and at that time,
they were not divided into groups by the speaker. I wish to see more
gifts so I feel why the speaker's gift is the favorite, if it truly is.

This draft is interesting. What hooked the writer into making this
list of moments is nowhere to be seen in this draft. The details set
the scene of the party economically, but perhaps too economically.
What were the gifts? When does the you say he loves everyone
there? The speaker says her gift is his favorite. How does she know?
And the last stanza. Is it sarcastic? Is there something beneath the
sarcasm that we can experience to actually feel why she is unbeliev-
ing and sardonic?

After our discussion, Bev rewrote:

More Than Anyone Else on Earth

The chairs leaned up against the wall
waiting for guests

my favorite music
your apprehension about the neighbors
then everyone arrives

the store bought cake with your name on it
everyone dances and then you open the gifts

a journal from me with a brown and tan Buddha
a sturdy cover
several versions of wine, savory foods
Starbuck's coffee, a poem,
a Buddha statue still warm from a pocket

Your ex-girlfriend gives you a blue cotton bag
hand sewn, with a tape of selected music in the pocket
and a handle long enough so the bag will fit closely to your body

Person by person you thank everyone
You say to her "I love you more than anyone else on earth"
and that's when I wish I were anyone else on earth
but me at your party

The title is fun (helping the writer relieve the sadness of the moment?) because for most of the poem, the reader thinks it applies to the unique place the you holds in the speaker's life. But by the poem's end, we know it also applies to the situation in which his words have put her. The champagne has disappeared from the poem. The chairs and music, cake and gifts tell enough to set the scene and emotional tone. The lines are so short and delicate that the matrix of this poem can't be burdened with unnecessary weight. The gifts are included with details that evoke them, the longest descriptions being those of the speaker's and ex-girlfriend's gifts. The details chosen to describe them certainly speak about the intimate place of each of these women in the you's life. This version doesn't back away from the emotional crisis of the you's faux pas. It brings that moment into being and leaves us there in the sad embarrassment that lingers and really can't be erased, though the you might want to erase it.

It is interesting to note that Judy worked from prose paragraph to long-lined poem, and Bev consistently worked with short lines in each draft. Sometimes you need to search broadly, margin to margin, for your poem, and sometimes it sings to you in short lines, but you have to make sure the lines are full of crisp images and doing the work of poetry. Either way works. What is important is that 1) the writer gets something written and can work from it, and 2) in working on the poem, the speaker manages to see the narrative strategy necessary to build the precise matrix into which the images will fit and transmit the poet's experience. In Bev's poem, the order of the details of the party set the scene and let time go by; from the chairs leaned up, music played, dances danced, cake out and gifts opened, the party progresses and builds toward the awkward moment. In Judy's poem, the event of preparing and canning the chutney and peach butter provided the narrative strategy.

Esther Altshul Helfgott, an experienced and prize-winning poet, agreed to work with my exercises. In the list of things she sees outside her window, Esther mentioned bird shit. After we discussed what emotional occasions might be "buried" in that image, she wrote this:

The Starlings

One day I'm going to wash the bird shit off the porch railing.
Then, I'll call a construction worker to seal up the holes
the birds use to make their nests in.

This has been going on for eight years now. Every season
when they've finished mating, hatching and raising their babies
I say I'm going to seal those damn holes up.

Sometimes I talk to them, ask why they have to pick the eves
of my house to live in. "It's not yours, you know, it's mine,"
I tell them, as the shit drops from the bird with the worm in its
     mouth.

Esther wrote this quickly and was amazed that I thought it was a poem. I do think it's a poem. She starts with what she sees, tells what action she threatens and never takes, and ends with the image of the bird eating and shitting, carrying on as normal. The poem seems to weigh more at the end than at the beginning. We move from a housekeeper's ambition to secure her home from nature's nuisance to a confrontation with nature in the form of one bird's action, which seems to stand for a larger issue—nature will win and have her way. Why fight the small stuff like patching the holes where birds make their nests? Doesn't everyone belong here? We see why the standoff has been going on for eight years, and we feel perhaps the writing of this poem will end the standoff with the birds and the poet, because of her acceptance of nature, winning.

William Stafford often told students he wrote a poem everyday. He just got up and wrote one each morning. Some were better than others, he said, but the secret to his writing was writing every day and not worrying about it. It may be intimidating to find and trust a daily poetic voice, and so you hesitate to write a poem a day. But you can certainly do lists each day, gaining in your ability to record details and images. You can create a store of material that, looked into honestly and perhaps with a trusted reader-responder, can yield an idea of the emotional occasions you are interested in writing from. Then you must 1) delve into the specific occasions with trust in the images each provides for your writing, and 2) take an interest in discovering the narrative structure each occasion chooses for its images.

SHAPING POEMS FROM SENSORY DETAILS

John Holmes, in *Writing Poetry*, says the poet:

> receives the world through his own heightened senses, and because one of them is a sense for words and their most exciting and most beautiful order, he transmits the world to all who will read poetry. He transmits the world alive, even more alive than in reality. Poetry is a great reserve of life on which we may draw when our own supply is low.

How do poets use their sense of how words work to communicate heightened experiences of the world? Let's look at several new poets' work using the exercises on sensory detail presented in chapter four.

Mirror Exercise

Here is an example of how someone may feel she is using words to capture a heightened sense of the world, but actually isn't. New

poet Liz Gamberg wrote this in response to the exercise about looking in the mirror and describing what you see without using
adjectives:

> *Who I See in the Mirror When I Look Into It*
>
> I see a mystery.
> I see silent rage.
> I see someone new.
> I see hair and fatigue and humor.

The words "mystery," "silent rage," and "new" cover a lot of ground
and so may seem heightened, but because they carry no specifics with
them, they flatten rather than heighten. What do you see that you
think is mysterious? What do you see that means silent rage? What
makes someone look new? Silent is an adjective modifying rage. Since
we can't see or hear the specific rage of the speaker, the word silent
doesn't carry any resonance or do any work for the writer. In fact, silent
rage is something of a cliché. We know it means the person is pent
up, but we don't know what that looks like, what we'd see if we looked
into the face. What does the hair look like? What does the fatigue look
like? The humor? Contrast the work above with its reliance on "big"
words and notions to the following work.

Photograph Exercise

Bev Parsons wrote the following in response to showing in words,
without relying heavily on adjectives, a person in a photograph. She
does use one adjective in the opening line and one in the last. However, they don't detract because they are only two adjectives in six
lines. I'll discuss one other important reason after you've read Bev's
response:

> *Photo of My Boyfriend in the Mountains*
>
> A ham smile on his face
> fog donning his cap
> his eyes tell
> this is the only place he should be
> Hills behind him grow with moss
> the stone wall is strong behind his knees

The words "ham" in the first line and "stone" in the last line are adjectives, but they go so seamlessly with the words they modify that they do not drain the energy from the sensory experience. Actually, they add information because they are specific, sensory words. The poem involves our senses with the fog, the cap, the hills with moss and the knees in front of a stone wall. This person is "backed up" by the environment he's in and he comes into his true texture there.

Here is another sight vignette by Bev, this one done from the exercise to describe who she saw in the mirror.

Who I See in the Mirror

Her hair lays easily on her shoulders
eyes are deep brown and black,
with circles under them Mom always complains about
can't you do anything about those circles
lips cracked from an all night wide open mouth

The last line tells us she can't do anything about those circles. The difficulty breathing at night shows in her face, on her lips, under her eyes. The juxtaposition of the cracked lips of the present with the question from the past causes a sense of poignancy. The speaker can't do anything about this (and probably so much more) that will improve her in her mother's eyes. Something striking, ever present and with a lot of history is strongly evoked here using sight images.

Again, brown and black are adjectives but they go so seamlessly with eyes and with the moment of looking into the mirror that they help rather than hinder her in getting to the direct experience. "All night wide open" is a phrase that behaves like an adjective, but again, so much experience is included we are drawn closer to the speaker.

SIMPLY SPECIFICS

What can Liz do to work on her sight detail and offer her writing the nutrition to grow a poem? She can go back to those words "mystery," "rage" and "new" and substitute things the eye can really see that may evoke experiences of mystery, rage and newness. But those words are so different from one another in emotional content that it would probably be a better idea to just go to the mirror and describe what she sees in simple specifics—and what she sees has some background behind the face or figure. Details of the background could certainly be included. The list "hair and fatigue and humor" is interesting because it contains items at different levels of abstraction; hair is more concrete than fatigue and humor. I think the word hair was the writer's unconscious telling her to get down to specifics. It is in specifics that the emotional occasion of a poem comes into being. "No ideas but in things," William Carlos Williams said. In the same vein, Wallace Stevens wrote, "Accuracy of observation is the equivalent of accuracy of thinking."

After we talked about her laconic lines, Liz decided she would keep going. But she first stopped to do a list she devised, a list of "what stands between me and my poems." Here is what she wrote:

> what stands between me
> and my poems is
> how good I am at fitting
> into small spaces, child's clothes,
> Dana's little rocking chair
> navigating narrow pathways
> on tiptoe in the woods,
> I step so softly
> even the birds don't fly away

To have a presence in a poem, the writer must be willing to put images of the world she sees in the lines. Liz has done that here, so now nothing stands between her and her poems.

When she went back to the mirror exercise, she wrote:

1. I see eyes that carry the length of this day, match my sea green sweater
2. I see my hair which has a mind of its own
3. I see my grandmother, Rose
4. I see the quilt N. made me for my 40th birthday, her own interpretation of a pattern called Chinese Coins
5. Antennae for my TV, so top-heavy, look like they could topple the TV
6. Red lips—feels like they'll be chapped forever
7. Dust on the mirror—I never clean it
8. Mole on the back of my hand, which is holding up my head

In this list are so many tangibles that could stand for her emotional feelings about herself in the world. We talked about the phrases "length of the day," "mind of its own," "grandmother Rose" and "Chinese Coins." Each of these could be more specific. Working on these details, Liz wrote:

I see my eyes sitting quietly near the back of my head,
tired from looking at 2 computers, tired from being in an office
with no windows all day.

I see my hair, dark and curly and going different ways
depending on the day. I inherited my father's hair genes.
When he had hair, it was black and thick and curly.
My mother's is fine and straight and it's been dyed
for so long, I don't know what it really looks like.
I just did one of those Clairol Natural Essence rinses for the first
    time.
I sort of feel like a liar—covering up my gray. I vowed I'd never
    do it,
never be self-conscious about aging, and here I am, self-conscious.
Oh no, I am my mother.

I see my grandmother Rose. Two of my favorite photos from
    babyhood
are of me with Rose. I look so happy, healthy with her—and I can
    see
how I resemble her. Blue eyes, dark hair with red in it. She looks
    so
happy being with me, feeding me as I am stuffed into my little
    chair. I
wish I felt healthy, hearty now. I don't. And I feel nervous about
what's going on in my body.

I see the quilt Nancy made me for my 40th birthday—her own
interpretation of a pattern called Chinese Coins. Traditionally a
    simple
pattern, red rectangles appliquéd on a white background, with a
    coin tied

to each rectangle along with intricate stitching. Nancy used various
materials, Balinese, tie-dye, reminiscent of fire and water, against
dark
rich blue. No coins. Such detailed perfect quilting.

LOOKING FOR OCCASION IN GENERATIVE WRITING

When I read this generative writing I like repeating Liz's words,
"When he had hair, it was black and thick and curly." (Generative
writing is the phrase I sometimes use to identify the exercise result
that is loaded with possibilities but doesn't look like a poem yet.)
It seems interesting to me that the writer sees her own hair "going
different ways" like her father's, while she sees her mother's hair
as straight, all in one direction and dyed so Liz doesn't know what
it looks like. I think she's got some energy behind a poem called
"My Father's Hair," which could ultimately include her own and
her mother's, or the energy may be in investigating how she sees
her father, mother and grandmother in her own image. Another occasion may be the quilt with no coins. What does that represent to the
poet? Something missing or something gained? Or both?

I use my sense of where the lively rhythms and images are in the
generative writing to guide new writers toward their poems. I also
read for repetition of concerns. Here Liz has included a lot of body
imagery—eyes, hair, concerns for health. She will have to decide if
the fatigue was the surface nonpoet in her just putting stuff on
paper or if an occasion about fatigue intrigues her. My guess is the
resonance is with the father's lively hair.

Here is what Liz gave me next:

> When he had hair, it was thick and black with curls too tight to let
>   the wind through.
> Eight millimeter home movies remind me that his body was
>   thicker then, that
> his skin had all its pigment—no white spots turned pink by hot
>   summer sun.
> It's almost like his hair was a cap keeping him in his body. He's
>   less body
> now—walks lightly. At 72, agile as he ever was.
>
> I have mistaken his silence for almost everything—true quiet,

judgment, not caring, shyness, transcendence. This life has been
    one
of sacrifice. He's made an art of it—mastering silence, absence,
walking away from physical pleasure, doing without. Discipline is
    his
ally. When he found out smoking was bad for him, he quit. I have
learned the power of renunciation from him.

Some memories:
I remember him telling me he used to drag his friends to hear
    classical
music—once to hear Jascha Heifetz. Not enough seats left, so they
    sat
up on the side of the stage. I wonder where that music touched
    him?

We had a nightly ritual of him wrapping me up like an egg roll in
    a thin
peach wool blanket. It had a large hole at its center where my feet
    had
been.

I am trying to remember how much hair he had when he came
    into my
bedroom early one morning . . . I began every day on the heating
    vent
warming my sleepy body, my school clothes suspended by the
    forced air
blowing through vents—each piece a little hot air balloon. He came
    to
tell me Uncle David's plane had crashed. I think he cried. I know
    the
death of his only brother sent ripples through all of us.

One evening I went into my parents' room for some candy. I was
    wearing
a yellow Swiss dot skirt with a flowered print blouse. Maybe I was
    12
years old. He said, "You're getting to be as big as a house." My
    stick

figure child's body was beginning to fill out, to take up a little
space. His words slammed me, reverberating for years. Little does
   he
know that I can remember each one clearly like peals of a bell,
   feel
them in my body which doesn't feel like it has a right to take up
   space.

I am very fond of the added phrase in the first sentence of Liz's
meditation, "with curls too tight to let the wind through." This writing
is not only evocative of the hair, but of a person's way of experiencing
someone else's hair. Additionally, the image of wind not getting
through helps the reader think of time passing and a lack of openness
to change. It is interesting, though, that Liz's mind decides not to
trust her evocation and goes instead to proof—the home movies—and
changes the subject from hair to skin and body build.

This happens a lot when we write: The rational left brain feels
left out and butts into things just when the design-oriented right
brain is making connections through the senses that need no explaining. Here, though, the right brain doesn't give up so easily and
enters again: "It's almost like his hair was a cap keeping him in his
body." Again, an image is given that evokes resistance, a fear of
vulnerability and connection. Then the left brain speaks, reasonably
but beside the poetic point, "He's less body now—walks lightly"
and so on. Then in the list of memories, the right brain evokes the
childhood memory of being wrapped like an eggroll and then goes
back to the point, "I am trying to remember how much hair he had
when he came into my bedroom early one morning." This leads to
the news of the plane crash and his brother's death. From there the
right brain thinks of another loss, the one of the father's seeming
lack of acceptance of his young daughter's growing up. The camara-
derie that existed, embodied in the image of being small and
wrapped up like an eggroll, is lost.

Based on my reading of where the right brain was headed with
this poem, I suggested the following rewrite to Liz:

My Father's Hair Was a Cap Keeping His Body In

When he had hair, it was thick and black,
the curls too tight to let the wind through.

I am trying to remember how much hair
he had when he came to my bedroom one morning
to tell me Uncle David's plane had crashed.
I think he cried.

I am trying to remember how much hair
he had when one evening, I went into my parents'
room for some candy. I wore a yellow Swiss
dot skirt with a flowered print blouse. I was 12.
He mistook my stick figure child's body
beginning to fill out for weight gain, said
I was getting big as a house.

And now I remember the early ritual of him
wrapping me up like an egg roll in a thin
peach blanket, the large hole at its center
where my feet had been.

I added a repetition of Liz's phrase, "I am trying to remember," to string the important images of the poem together. This structure keeps the reader in touch with the speaker as she remembers her father's hair. She then revised the last stanza to begin with, "And now I remember. . . ."

♦ ♦ ♦

For Bev, the narrative occasion was built in—looking at a photo or looking into the mirror. The emotional occasion or feeling amassed from what she reported seeing came from the details and images selected by her unconscious. In Liz's poem, the narrative occasion grows from the repetition of "I am trying to remember." When you write, trust that your unconscious will. It organizes around the occasion presented in an exercise. But if you don't feel that happening in your writing, write too much. Keep going like Liz ultimately did, telling what you see in direct, specific language. You will probably find that certain details and images go together to create a pool of feeling, and others are coming from some other story all together. Prune the strays away and you will have something to work with.

CHAPTER SEVEN

Shaping Poems From More Beginnings

It is necessary to any originality to have the courage to be an amateur.
　　　—*Wallace Stevens*
　　　from "Adagio"

A poet is aware of sound as being integral to the heart's message. Hard sounds offer one message, soft sounds another. Consonants inherently tell us of feelings by comparing them to footsteps or an ax hitting a log. Vowels sing to us of emotional weather, of longing, of a saw moving through wood. When a poet trusts her images and occasion, the sounds in her poem sing the tune of the poet's perception and world. Practicing with the tool of sound makes the poet more sensitive to using it well in writing poetry.

SOUNDS

By consciously working with alliteration in the sound sensory exercises, Judy Tough wrote this:

> *Waiting on a Corner in Prague for the Bus*
> *to Take Us Back to Our Rented Apartment*

> Honking hulk hitched to hamstrings hovering high above, take me
> to my holiday home.

With the words repeatedly starting with *h*, we get the emotional picture of this streetcar as it appeared to the speaker, who is a stranger in Prague. The *h*'s seem to hush a fear of or discomfort with the strangeness of a foreign place; the repeated hushes help the speaker control any uncomfortable feelings. We hear the foreignness of this home in the repeated *h*'s, but we also sense from the denotation of the words "holiday" and "home" that it will be a relief and comfort to get safely back to it.

Sounds of a Kitchen

Judy also played with onomatopoeia and transcribed this:

In My Kitchen
Making Bagel Dough in My New Bread Machine

Cunk, cunk, cunk....cunk, cunk, cunk....cunk, cunk, cunk...knock,
   knock, knock,
knock, knock, knock, knock, knock, knock, knock.....knock,
   knock, knock....knock,
knock, knock....knock, knock, knock...........beep, beep,
   beep.........bip,
bip.....bip, bip....bip, bip....bip, bip....bip, bip.....knock, knock,
   knock, knock,
knock..

Judy was noticing the kinds of sounds, the pattern of repetition and the spacing of the sounds. She was training her ear. In our sight-dominated culture, taking time to listen to the world is important when learning how to add dimension to your poetic voice. Heightening your sense of sound allows you to speak your perceptions and truth in rhythm and words that transmit your genuine experience.

Mixing Sound Play Into the Other Exercises

New poet Terry Chambers did one of the listing exercises as he played with alliteration. He was working on the list of jobs he would like to have and what he would wear. Here is one job. As you read, listen for his use of alliteration.

Dream Job for My Soul

I'd like to be an archaeologist
excavating the floor of a shallow cave in a red
rock cliff in a canyon in New Mexico.

I'd dress like an adventurer of the "old school,"
khaki shorts with lots of pockets, a floppy canvas
hat with ventilation holes around the top.

I'd grow a big beard for the job with grizzly
gray patches in it, and I'd wear glasses—the kind
that tint in the sun and clear in the darkness of the cave.

Listen to the *c*, *k* and *r* sounds in the first stanza. The phrase "red rock cliff in a canyon" seems to swoop up the sounds from the earlier part (aRchaeologist, exCavating, Cave) and cement them together just as the speaker's vision is cementing together.

In the second stanza, he knows how he'd look—old school, lots of pockets, ventilation holes in his hat. Although the contiguous words do not start with the same sound, "I'd dress" has the repeated *d* sound, and "dress," "school," "shorts," "pockets," "canvas" and "holes" all have *s* sounds. There is something ongoing in *s* sounds, like air escaping—his pent-up soul is bursting through.

The third stanza returns to strict alliteration: big beard, grizzly gray. The *g* sounds gain force with the word "glasses." The stanza also contains those *s* sounds of escape (patches, glasses, sun, darkness), and the *c* and *r* sounds that transmit the quality of sureness (clear and cave). The speaker was merely inventing a description of the job he would like and what he would wear. But because he was sensitive to sound, the true emotional occasion—the soul making clear how it works in this world—came through. The soul needs to see in the dark (the glasses are clear there), but not be so in the dark ("a shallow cave") that it can't come up to the light. The soul needs pockets to hold what it has experienced, and certainly ventilation holes in a hat can only help as things heat up!

SMELL

The sense of smell is underused in poetry, but it is a sense that brings us to our experience. Bev Parsons wrote short responses on the smells of learning, being lost and reading a beloved book:

Remembering the feeling that I could write poetry
smelled like fresh laundry on a cool sunny day

Being lost in Washington DC smelled like too much lavender
soaked into my clothes; I just wanted to get away from it
As I read my favorite book the moment smells of baby powder.

Playing with the exercise this way will give you practice getting
sensory information into your poem. The results can be used to
"thicken the brew" as Ron Hanson calls this approach in his contribu-
tion to *The Writer's Journal: 40 Contemporary Writers and Their Journals*.

Imagining the Smell of Someone's Anger You Have Experienced

New poet Denise Benitez wrote the following, which was inspired by the smell exercise about anger:

> My mother's anger smells like those potted narcissus that
> someone gives you in the fall pretending to be sweet, but
> really they smell like rotting garbage. Like a rat that has
> died under the floor. You don't want to get too near but
> you don't want to throw them away, they're so pretty!
>
> Some secret bulb heart that isn't a real flower—so
> small and white and innocent and the smell could knock
> you on your back.

I think this is off to an evocative start that makes me feel approach
and avoidance. Something is pretty sickening under the guise of
smelling sweet. But is it the mother's anger or the poet's at her
mother? I advised Denise to describe her anger by either writing
more stanzas starting with smells or other senses, or writing one
sense to a stanza. Or she could move from the sense of smell into a
direct address. She could start with, "Mother, . . . " and then write
from memories of her mother being angry at her.

Here is Denise's next draft:

> *Narcissus*
>
> My mother's anger smells like
>   those potted narcissus that
> pretend to be so sweet. They're small
>   and white and innocent,
> but don't get too near,

there is something rotting here, there is
some secret bulb heart that is not a real
flower.

Mother your anger was too pretty and delicate
    to shield my sister and me from the slap of his
belt on tender young skin, from the sting of his
    hand across our faces, from his cold stares endured
    at dinner time.
So many high heels in the closet, all that makeup,
    so many dresses, bright flowers of cheap longing
and the dream of living another life than this one.
The life where the flowers truly do smell sweet and
    your claws come out, your heart pumps like a wildcat
and you rake his powerful body
to shreds.

I am struck by the wonderful new images—the pretty high heels
and dresses with their flowers of cheap longing. I am struck by the
claws and wildcat heart (the rat transformed into a tiger or bobcat
or lion). So much so that if it were my poem, I would reverse the
order of the stanzas and let the speaker speak directly to the mother
from the start. The imge of the dream and its possible absence
evokes the "secret bulb heart" so well that the phrase isn't necessary
any more. "Not a real flower" was probably the language that got
Denise's unconscious to deliver the stronger, more surprising, more
evocative "flowers of cheap longing."

> *Narcissus*

Mother, you never shielded my sister
and me from the slap of his belt on tender
young skin, from the sting of his hand across our faces,
from his cold stares endured at dinner.

So many high heels in the closet, all that
makeup, so many dresses, bright flowers
of cheap longing. Did you ever dream another life
where your claws came out, your heart pumped
like a wildcat and you raked his powerful body to shreds?

If not, whatever anger you pretend is a potted
narcissus, shallow rooted and pretty for the moment,
its sweet fragrance like fruit beginning to rot.

Published poet Gary Winans did the exercise by thinking of the
smell of his father's anger:

He told us no walnuts—no messing with them, green
shelled, sticky, resinous walnuts—but we rode our bikes
up E. Ave. to Mrs. Black's corner of E. Ave. and Morgan,
among the windfall—lined them up across the avenue &
waited for cars topping the hill—couldn't stop in time,
broke open the nuts which we picked up and they stained
our hands bitter black pitch color.

   Arriving at the wood screen door, he met us—tried to
cuff the backs of our butch haircut heads—we ducked
and he sent us to our room to be punished. His anger
smelled of fresh leather he would use on our bottoms
once, twice, three times—crack of sweat drenched belt—
but he never did, never came down the hall. We punished
ourselves enough he knew pacing our room rubbing bitter
palms on stained, acid sweaty jeans.

When I asked Gary to see if he could begin to shape a poem from
this experience, he wrote:

Only Once Did Dad Hit Us, or Try To

he told us: no walnuts—no messing with them,
green shelled, sticky, resinous black walnuts,
but we rode our bikes up to East Avenue by Mrs. Blacks
where we knew we would find a windfall of walnuts
alongside Poorman Schoolhouse
on the north side of the hill.
we lined up hard shelled walnuts like a trail of ants, perpendicular
to the north bound cars coming over the crest of the hill.
they couldn't stop in time and crossed
our row of nuts, gnashing, popping, broke them open as we
couldn't with large stones or a piece of firewood
and scooped up the hulls and meat

and reset the line with young-boy dashes
back and forth across the asphalt road,
our hands stained a bitter green
that changed with the evening light
to a black pitch.
waiting at the side door when we arrived home
late for dinner, Dad took one look at our stained hands
and tried to cuff the backs of our butch hair cuts
as we went through the wood-screen door he held
but we ducked and he sent us to our room
to be punished.
fear was a chill of nervous sweat.
anger was the smell of the leather belt he said
he'd crack once, twice, thrice
across our stained dungarees.
but he never did,
never came down the hall;
he knew the longer we waited
trying to rub our bitter sweaty palms clean
on stained acrid jeans
the more we punished ourselves.

My favorite images are of the boys lining the walnuts up in a row
like ants and their young-boy dashes into the street to retrieve the
car-cracked nuts. I like "reset the line" very much, too. These images made it into this second draft because Gary, affirmed that his
memory was a poem-in-the-making, was willing to put even more
of his experience on the page. To find the most interesting parts of
the story, he used the tools of compression and placing interesting
words to start and end lines. He dropped words that were less interesting and fixed the grammar so it moved the narration in the poem
along more smoothly.

Here is his vivid and evocative poem about a young boy's life
and the way feelings linger into adulthood:

We Rode Our Bikes Up to East Avenue by Mrs. Blacks'

Where we knew we would find a windfall of walnuts
alongside Poorman Schoolhouse on the north side of the hill.

We lined them up like a trail of ants perpendicular to the north
bound cars coming over the crest of the hill. They crossed
our row, gnashed, popped, broke them open as we could not
with large stones and firewood. We scooped the hulls and meat,
reset the line with young-boy dashes across the asphalt road.
In evening light, our hands turned black from bitter green.

When we arrived home late for dinner, Dad held the wood
screen door, tried to cuff the butch cut heads we ducked
and sent us to our rooms. The smell of his anger is
the belt leather he said he'd crack across our butts.
I still wipe sweaty palms across my jeans.

TASTE

Memory and experience are stored in all of our senses. We can remember experience when we taste something from that experience.
In order to evoke taste, we have to use words for things that we can
see, but we discuss them in a way that puts them in our mouths.
Wallace Stevens said, "The tongue is an eye."

The Taste of Intangibles

Thinking about the tastes of things, published poet Marilyn Meyer
described chocolate as tasting like an affair with someone who is already taken, because the flavor never lasts. She said tofu tastes like
drowsiness, and since it takes on the flavors of whatever it's cooked
with, it is "confused" and "has a short memory." She found out how
ignorance and anger taste for her. Ignorance, she said, tastes like a blue,
mango-flavored popsicle, chemically sweetened, artificially flavored.

She said anger tastes liked the fried liver she was forced to eat as
a child:

> Anger tastes like the fried liver I was force-fed as a child.
> Back then camouflage was my strategy. I'd cover those
> ashen piles, dry as potter's clay, cloak them in mashed
> potatoes, wrap them in a guise of petit peas, then dip
> them in ketchup red as wax lips. I'd swallow holding my
> breath, try to purge my palate with chocolate milk.

Thinking this taste of anger might be a useful metaphor for how
she handles her anger, Marilyn wrote:

In my twenties I used avoidance. When my husband cooked liver I'd cut it into rectangles, move them around with my fork, slyly slide them off my plate onto the dining room rug. Slivers flattened and gray stuck to my husband's shoes for days. I still hate liver, but these days I take my anger straight—face it, chew it, let the putrid taste bring tears to my eyes which burn.

Here Bev Parsons uses imagery to evoke taste:

Hate:
The taste of blood in my mouth as the dental hygienist cleans my
    teeth
Love:
The taste of ripe mango sloshing through my mouth
Laughter:
The taste of Indian spices; cardamom, cumin and cloves
Ignorance:
The taste of brown gravy that you thought was chocolate pudding
    in the fridge
Humiliation:
The taste of an artichoke when no one told you how to eat it

How Tangibles Lend Their Tastes

Although Bev did not develop this exercise into a poem, she was aware of her facility with specific detail when she did the "When I Saw You . . ." exercise and brought what she'd learned into her work. Note the things that have taste in this poem:

When I Saw You Packing to Go Away

You were counting
so sensitive and careful
3 essential sandwiches
2 bottles of water
1 eye shade
into a heavy blue duffel bag

Deep inside lay a little white bunny
we'd hidden from each other so often

soft ears
a thin gold collar
a pink nose

she mashed up easily when I squished her
into a place where I was sure you wouldn't look
You had planned a few things for me to do
clean and chop carrots
open battery packs
hold the bag while you zipped

Bev doesn't spell out what tastes like what, but she lists food items that belong to the narrative occasion stated by the title. The presence of these items and the poet's trust in them as integral to the moment sets the poem's readers up for tasting. By the end of the poem, we are tasting the feeling of being taken away from oneself when a loved one leaves.

TOUCH

When Terry Chambers sat down to add touch words to the list I presented in chapter four, he wrote, "slick, prickly, ragged, scaly, coarse, pocked, dripping with cold, piercing, supple, raw, alive and slick." He also wrote examples of what has these touch traits:

ragged and scaly as bark on a fir tree;
coarse as a door screen;
pocked like wind and water worn stone;
dripping with cold like the concrete pillars of the freeway bridge
    on a day when Seattle is soaked;
piercing as the hairs of cactus pad, a handful of razors, as dry blades
    of grass;
supple as old leather;
raw as a child's scraped knee;
alive and slick as a panicked fish or a puppy's kisses.

If you haven't done this, you might enjoy looking back at your list of touch words and naming specific things that feel that way—the more surprising, the better.

Terry thought about many of the images I asked about in chapter five. He wrote that sunlight on his arm while he is driving feels like "he is under the broiler." Bed sheets are "crisp and cool as sea water." He described how he slips into them and "sleeps like a snake with scales on his skin, buried deep in sand of the bank, of cool, cool river."

Terry wrote the following about one of the prompts I had supplied: "Tongue on my tongue—the very edge of the high waterfall, eager / and bursting to take the plunge, whirlpools of sweetness."

I like reading and experiencing this description of a kiss. My experience of bed sheets is refreshed by Terry's words. Poetry works by reactivating our sense experience of actions, objects, people, places and things.

Practicing with touch words and detailing how things feel helps you create the emotional space to build a poem. As with all of the senses, gaining skill in describing the sensations from things that touch and surround your body helps you keep the vitality of your experiences alive and enhances your ability to respond to occasions from which to write.

Gary Winans wrote the following poem after experiencing unusual heat in a western Washington summer. He had in mind the exercise where you describe the sounds in a park where you walk:

In the Joy of Shade

It's 100 degrees and the sun reigns now and we
almost drown in its brightness, slipping from one
shady oasis to the next, making our way across the state
park to the Candy Store, swimsuits, flipflops,
our brown skin needing something cool.

Pausing by cottonwoods and wild roses
limp in the shade of Campsite 47, I hear above the radios
blaring up off the beach and the RV generator revving up,
above the plague of midday jetskis whining, whining in pathetic
arcs over blue blue water: tree crickets.

Translucent lime-green insects, clinging to thin stem
refugia, as cool as tiny popsicles singing the joy of shade,
rhythmic song like a string of silver sleigh bells
rising and falling over some distant snow-cool hills.

The sensations of sun-heat and snow-cold form the frame of this poem. The heat prompts the desire to stay in the shade, and the observation in the shade prompts the cooling visualization. Although the poem skillfully relies on sound, the sense of touch prompts the occasion. This speaker is experiencing total immersion in the heat and can describe it to us: bathing suits drying like wicks and bodies like tallow. But once he hears the song of the lime-green insects, he can imagine popsicles (like the ones they are no doubt after in their walk to the store). From there the feel of cooling ice takes the speaker to visualizations of sleigh bells, which mean snow and colder weather.

Here is another of Gary's poems born of paying attention to touching:

> *Beneath the Stars*
>
> _lie !_
> we lay on our backs, side-by-side
> on a cool canvas-covered raft, tethered,
> floating on steel drums,
> a ladder dipping into the water,
> to our skiff.
>
> We are motionless
> except when we adjust our hands
>
> next to one another,
> except when a shooting star
> tilts our sky for a moment.
>
> We are trying to grasp what is beyond
> everything we see overhead.
> We imagine other worlds imagining us.
>
> We imagine everything known
> is like the raft
> and everything else
> keeps us afloat,
>
> and our only certainty
> is the cotton fabric
> failing to keep our sunwarmed skin
> from touching.

Your sense of touch can communicate your emotional perception of a situation. What you take in through the nerve endings of your skin, in your fingers, along your cheek or the entire length of your body has something to say. In the poem above, the awareness of the speaker's body touching the other's as they lie on the raft keeps the poem afloat. In the first stanza, they lie side by side in a small space covered with a cool canvas; in the second stanza, they adjust their adjacent hands; in the third stanza, their skin is touching. Here is a statement about being small and unknowing in the universe, but full with attraction, a love poem.

USING ALL OF THE SENSES

I want to share the results of another student's exercise in using four senses—taste, sound, smell and touch—to examine her anger at her mother.

Taste/Sound/Smell/Feel of My Anger

1) burnt stew, the way it burns in the bottom of the pot and when you're eating it you don't see the burnt part but the taste pervades. Invisible but there

2) smell of burnt hair

3) smell of a cast iron pot that's gotten too hot on the stove and the way the smell catches in your nostrils just as you're inhaling

4) siren getting louder and louder as a fire engine approaches

5) fingernails on a blackboard

6) doors slamming

7) being in really harsh sunlight with no shade for respite

8) telephone with the ringer turned up too loud

When I read this list, I asked my student when she had smelled burnt hair, hoping it might provide a way into a final form of this poem. She said that sometimes when she cooks, a strand of her hair falls onto the gas flame of a burner. Since such an occasion made her think of her mother, I suggested that she start by telling her mother that a strand of her hair had once again fallen into the gas burner's blue flame and it reminded her of her anger toward her mother. I also told her that the image of doors slamming might be a good ending because this kind of anger probably got in the way of closeness and listening between them. Here is her next draft:

Mother, a strand of my hair falls
into the blue flame as I cook tonight.
It fries in an instant, blue to brittle.
The smell lingers,
I turn on the wrong burner,
and you are in the stench of hot cast iron
that catches my throat
as I take my next breath
I set the table,
and you are the blue ice
hissing, cooling drinks in expensive glasses.
The telephone rings too loud
on the metal counter.
It is you.
You tell me to set you a place at this table.
I want to say you already are at this table.
I want to say you are already here.
I want to say this meal will never satisfy your hunger.

My first response to this version was to the strand of hair—I wanted
to linger with that image longer. How did it come to fall into the flame?
What did it look like? Or did the speaker miss seeing it and only know
it had fallen into the flame from the smell? Next, I wondered why so
much was going wrong in this cooking—hair in the flame, empty pot
on a heated burner. The writer seems to be in a state even before the
phone rings. The litany at the end about "I want to say" seems to
soften the anger beneath the poem. I'm rooting for the speaker to say
what she has to say because a poem offers that opportunity.

Here is the poet's revision after I shared my responses and after
she worked more with the section on metaphor in chapter four.

Mother, I lit the stove tonight
and before I placed the pot of soup
on the burner, a strand of my hair
fell into the blue flame
fried in an instant, brittle then vaporized,
a comet traveling towards the sun.
I choked on the smell, caught
in my throat like a mosquito
inhaled in summer woods.

I set the table and you were
the blue ice hissing, cooling down
the drinks. I counted out silverware,
and no matter how carefully
I placed the forks, knives,
and spoons beside each plate,
I heard the sound of windows breaking.

The phone rang too loud on the metal
counter. I knew it was you wanting
a place at this table.
I heard your claws, sharp
as thorns of a rose, trying to pry
open the door inside me
slammed shut years ago as I
sat at tables with housekeepers,
wondering if I would recognize you
when you returned from endless vacations.

I wouldn't even know where to seat
you at this table, yet you are already here.
No meal I make will satisfy the hunger.

How much more satisfying the narrative structure of this version
is. We can see the speaker cooking, putting the soup on the burner,
watching a hair burn like a comet blazing then gone, catching the
smell in her throat like a bug. With our feet planted in the preparation of the meal (we know it is soup and, with the smell imagery
streamlined to stay with the hair, the need to talk about a cast iron
pot has gone away), we can move more easily to the setting of the
table and the presence of the mother in the images. It is clear that
the daughter, who is cooking and setting the table for guests, is
remembering her mother and her feelings for her. When the phone
rings—loud because of the metal counter it sits on—and it is the
mother, we feel the synchronicity of the event (often when we are
thinking of someone, they suddenly call). By the third stanza, we
know, too, because of the speaker's saying rather than wanting to
say, what causes her anger and unease. The poem has begun to
weigh more at the end than at the beginning: The speaker's anger
and unease concerning her mother is heightened with the new com-

plexity of her sudden interest after years of not showing enough interest. Finally, the last line speaks of both their hungers, the mother's and the daughter's, and that is satisfying.

SHAPING POEMS WITH METAPHOR, SIMILE AND BANTU

John Holmes writes that "the poet comes equipped with a highly associative mind. He is forever likening, even if he has to reach back through years of muscular memory to make the connection." Practicing with the metaphor and simile exercises in chapter four can be essential to increasing the strength and speed with which you are able to use the likening muscle when you are in the midst of writing from an occasion.

Metaphor and Simile

In a poem written from the red rock cliffs of Zion Canyon, Terry Chambers was describing some of what he saw, borrowing just a little from the "nobody knows" exercise in chapter six:

> Everyone sees the current, but I see
> the leaves in the current, yellow aspen.
> On the surface, they are like butterfly wings
> but they go deep and vanish
> as though into the mouth of a trout.

Terry can evoke a lot visually and emotionally by using similes. Although the leaves look like they might fly away like butterflies, they disappear in the current as food might into the mouth of a trout. We know what that disappearing looks like. Because it is specific, it is more resonant than a general disappearing into a current. In this particular disappearing, the leaves are part of the life of the current, a nutrition, not just devoured. There is an implied purpose and cycle to their disappearance. If Terry were to continue writing from this occasion, he might discover what this way of viewing nature was allowing him to see about himself.

Practicing with metaphor and simile helped Gary Winans write from the occasion of a late-night phone call from a lover who was slipping out of his life. He was prepared to use analogical thinking because he'd done metaphor exercises for years:

It's Over

She said I'll call you. And now it was over
or so she'd implied. Yet she hadn't taken her TV
or the pole lamp with the chipped enamel edges, so I clung
to hope and hovered by day within ear distance of the phone,
dragging it by its long cord to the kitchen while I cooked,
to the middle of the room while I stretched before going to bed.
I slept in pensive, restless threshold-plunges
suffering change-in-life suspense.

When her call awakened me, I grabbed for an opaque
plane-tail disappearing into fog. She got to the point as always
saying, "Those fuckers, I can't stand 'em," as three digits
dropped like heavy eyelids to 4:00 on my old Sears clock.

I understand this hate of rodents: Where dreams should be floating
overhead in whispers of desire, she hears only late night
furtive toenails scratching on the rafters. "I set traps," she said.
What kind of bait? "Peanut butter." *Good choice.*

The background noise on the phone changes. She is pacing
around her house, past the piano in the living room to her empty
guest bedroom, talking to me on a cordless phone.
You may have winged one. I picture a gray shape like a fur-lined
glove twisted inside out dragging by a leg, crushed
in a copper colored spring. She hangs up.

I notice how the street light pales the navy curtains
around my window. I think how I forgot to tell her
you can tie a trap to the floor and tether it
like a lover to the phone.

The phone like a plane's tail and the clock's numbers like heavy
eyelids are metaphors that evoke coming out of sleep. Finally, the
lover tethered to the phone like a trap to the floor makes the imagery
the poet sees complete. The dead rodent like a gray glove inside
out begins to turn attention toward a human abandoned like a glove
taken off. The story in the poem moves in such a way that the poet
can articulate his situation rather than just live it over and over. The

occasion of the phone call and its content prompts the poet to tell the story of his condition. The use of two well-chosen similes get the gears oiled and moving. The emotional and narrative occasions kludge together in the last analogy: The speaker is not caught, but very, very trapped. The she is on a cordless phone, but he drags a long cord around wherever he goes!

Bantu

Before we head into the next chapter and explore results from the exercises in chapter five, notice how facility with the African two-line form bantu can help the poet.

Terry Chambers created these bantus:

> Gold toothed Neils sits down at the poker table
> Gypsy around the campfire

> Nya nurses my grandson
> golden melon from a strong brown vine

> Hot tea on a murky, stormy night
> Red hot chilies

Writing lines that juxtapose sight, sound, taste, smell or touch images keeps us prepared to incorporate just the right images in just the right phrases on any poem's particular occasion. To see this, let's look at another poem by Bev Parsons:

> *Writing Here at Olympic Pizza*

> I take myself to these places late at night
> so someone will feed me. I take no food at home.

> Two and a half months is a long time for a partner's
> absence, no one to remind me of body and love.

> I cherish these moments, the depth of my pain,
> the fog that hangs in the night.

> Someone is waiting for me. I wait and I wait.
> Is it you? Are you the one who wants me?

Again, Bev's poem is economical and lyrical in its sound and slight images. But it is perfectly clear in its narrative as well—a woman is writing in a pizza house late at night, mourning the absence of her partner, feeling her loss and wondering if he will be back. "The depth of my pain, the fog that hangs in the night" could be a bantu if it were all by itself. It slips in here beautifully to evoke the feelings of the speaker.

Liz Gamberg wrote the following bantus:

> the back of my hands
> dried riverbeds
>
> steam from an iron
> someone yawning
>
> safety pins on your housedress
> medals of honor
>
> colors of your dresses
> ocean, grass, sky
>
> wind blowing through tree leaves
> someone waving hello to me

Liz was specifically remembering Rena, a housekeeper from her childhood, as she generated these bantu. Here is how she incorporated these images into a poem:

> *There Are Days When Wind Blows*
> *and the Leaves Are Your Hands Waving to Me*
> for Rena
>
> I look at the back of my hands, dried
> riverbeds and wonder what you saw in yours
> as you labored twenty years in our home, childless
> and seven states away from your husband.
>
> Afternoons I'd return from school and watch
> you watching soap operas and ironing creases
> into and out of anything, while steam yawned
> then hung in the air against our skin like pillows.

Part of what I knew those years was that
your fried chicken would grace our dinner table
once every week, that the color of a dress
could match ocean, grass, or sky, that on you
safety pins were medals where buttons used to be.

Did you know I was like a bird nesting in your thick
black branches, hoping even when a moon
was new, I could find the way home to you?

◆ ◆ ◆

Shaping poems from your beginnings means looking into the material you created using the tools of the trade and finding: 1) the occasion, both physical and emotional, upon which you are wanting to write, and 2) the lyric and narrative values you can use in your work. Then heighten your use of both. This means: 1) replacing ineffective summarizing and judgmental words with specifics; 2) placing strong words at the beginning and ending of most of your lines; 3) allowing your senses of sight, sound, taste, smell and touch into your writing; and 4) using the associative language of metaphor, simile and bantu to show experience.

Practice gets you to success. Write and write; shape and shape!

CHAPTER EIGHT

Using the Poet's Stance for Writing Personal Poetry

. . . perhaps all the dragons of our lives are princesses who are only waiting to see us once beautiful and brave.
—Rainer Maria Rilke
Letters to a Young Poet

Psychologist and scholar James Hillman investigates genius or calling in his book entitled *The Soul's Code: In Search of Character and Calling.* He is convinced that each of us is born with an "acorn" or image of our calling and we spend our lives unfolding toward it or driven by it. As described in Plato's *Republic* and in several mystical religions, a daimon, Hillman says, comes to earth with each of us, assigned to see that we fulfill our purpose and live our pattern. For body and soul to do this, though, requires a growing down into the physical, human world:

> The heart's image requires efforts of *attachment* to every sort of anchoring circumstance, whether these anchors be the loyalty of friends, the stability of contracts, the reliability of health, the schedules of the clock, the facts of geography . . . there can never be enough world in which to sink its roots.

The work of the poet, it seems to me, is to discover the heart's (or poem's) image and transmit this awareness through the details of daily actions, voices, homes, towns and events. To do this, the poet must find a way into the mundane that locates the soul's world of correspondences, of timelessness within time, of loneliness for something the heart remembers.

Each of the exercises in chapter five included a strategy that placed the writer in a poet's stance toward the world. In the next two chapters, we'll look at the results of new and experienced poets' work with these exercises. We'll see how, these poets created landscapes that reveal the "world within this world" by using the poet's stance. We'll listen for the way rhythm, rhyme, line breaks, compression, diction and tone participate in creating a precise articulation of perception and feeling.

NOBODY KNOWS

In my example in chapter five, I suggested clustering from four phrases. New poet Meg Agnew did a cluster (see page 112) around the phrase "happy situation." She wrote it in the center of a blank page in her spiral-bound notebook.

The item in her cluster that drew her attention was "seeing the finches in the pear tree." Using her own version of the "I didn't" and "I did" prompts I suggested in chapter five, Meg wrote:

Seeing the Finches

I didn't imagine it. The finches
    were laughing as
    they swooped around the garage and
    into the branches of the pear tree.

I didn't see if there were five or six
    of them.

I didn't breathe. They were so close to
    royalty, celebrities and me
    just for an instant hidden
    in the leaves.

From this point, Meg looked at what it would take to more fully evoke the gaiety of the scene, the heart-lifting joy of being a close observer of nature's bounty and happy activity. Here is her revision:

A Party of Finches

I didn't imagine it. The finches, 5 or 6 of them,
were laughing as they swooped around the corner

of the house and in among the pear tree branches
where I stood, pruning shears in hand.

They flew so close, I held my breath and watched
these small celebrities until they noticed me,
                        half-hidden in the leaves.

But even my unwelcome presence failed to curb
    their gaiety   as they went singing, soaring off
and left me, bereft of feathers, without wings.

The title now gives us a feeling tone. The "I didn't" prompt that remains alerts us to how easily the speaker might have overridden the value of participating in this moment, and how we must give credence to our senses. The recording that there were five or six finches shows us that the precision in this observation is about feeling, not science. Having discovered the intruder, the birds leave freely, their emotions unchanged, but the speaker is aware of lacking something. The spacing before "half-hidden in the leaves" seems to reflect a hiding, something secret. The spacing around "their gaiety" indicates this may be the part others would think the speaker imagined.

Look for rhyming and half-rhyming words to see how they contribute to the feeling tone of the poem. "Celebrities" and "me" are in one line and the rhyme furthers the connection between the speaker and the birds. Then in, "failed to curb / their gaiety   as they went singing, soaring off," the vowel sounds in "curb" and "off" do not rhyme, reinforcing the feeling that the speaker, not the birds, is curbed and apart from nature. Rather than trying to rhyme as you write, become attentive in revision to where the rhymes are and are not, and how they serve the poem. If you feel they sound right and are not distracting or chiming, it is the soul talking, allowing you to experience yourself in the moment. Meg has captured the difference between humans and the rest of the animate world, a perception that may have gone unwritten but for her memory of seeing the finches as a happy situation. She shows us how writing a scene with simple words can form the vessel through which the soul-connecting moment is made.

A cluster is a personal intuitive, associative mining of the self for images from which to write. While the images in Liz Gamberg's cluster (see page 114) are not mentioned specifically in the poem, they informed her choice of metaphor.

> I didn't say I can hardly see the stars when I talk to you.
> I didn't see that your words caught me like thorns of a rose.
> I didn't tell the truth.
>
> I said there was somewhere I had to be.
> I saw myself shrivel.
> I slithered through the rest of day.

This short poem is evocative of the effect lying has on oneself when it would be more freeing to tell the truth. I asked Liz for a title and to look again at her first line. What would make the stars hard to see? Could she share that image? Here is her revision:

When You Called

I didn't say I see fog obscure the stars when I talk to you.
I didn't see that your words caught me like thorns of a rose.
I didn't tell the truth.

I said there was somewhere I had to be.
I saw myself shrivel.
I slithered through the rest of day.

One of the ways the design, or emotional mind, is cultivated for its knowledge is through sound. In this poem, leaving the prompts in allows the writer to use a repetition of sound to come up with the important word "slithered," which is at the heart of the poem's meaning. Here is the work Terry Chambers's drafted using the same prompts from chapter five. His cluster is on page 116.

I didn't get on his case when he
didn't hang up the kayaks.
I didn't complain when he stood us up
for two dinner dates.
I didn't say, "Hey, you've owed me that
$250 for more than a year. You say
you're going to work it off, but then you
never help me do anything. What kind of
garbage is this?"
I didn't say, "How about some respect?
You're supposed to respect your father; you're
supposed to be honest with me and helpful."
I didn't say, "Dope smoking is making
you brain dead. You're becoming an irresponsible
jerk like Patrick. You've become self-centered
and withdrawn, etc."
I didn't get on his case about
education. He enjoys being ignorant. "You
didn't even graduate from high school; what's
your own son going to think of you when
he grows up?" I didn't say, "If you don't
respect me, what will your own son say
about his dope smoking redneck dad?"

I didn't say this, but I thought it
and I've kept it to myself.
 I didn't give him that last $50
for the power bill. I didn't rescue last
time, and I haven't heard from him
since either.

 I did call the lawyer and get
the house deal down on paper.
 I did make it clear about what
his obligations are, payments he must
make etc. And that feels good.
 I did tell him I thought
 smoking dope and
 whitewater kayaking
 down the river
 don't mix.
I did tell him it was time
to think of Nya and
the baby,
life insurance that sort of boring
responsible sort of thing
and I did
tell him I have expectations
he has obligations . . .
time to be a grown-up
daddy now
that he has family of his own.
Maybe this is how the
message goes
from father son
to father son
like a stick
that tumbles
down the rapids
like a kayak shell
that tumbles through white water
from level through level
down through generations.
Maybe a young man needs

that kind of turbulence
out of his boat
in white water
hoping to break free.

My first question to Terry Chambers was why it was important to
have had the kayaks hung up, and my first advice was to create a title.
The answer to my question resulted in a title that cites the occasion
that prompted the speaker to speak. My next advice was to think about
writing in longer lines. David Wagoner teaches that long lines help a
poet gain momentum, and short lines help a poet make the reader
pause and go slower. When working on revisions, think about whether
your poem needs a reader to move along more quickly or more slowly
and why. In this case, longer lines build the momentum to a "bawling
out" or "letting off steam" that this occasion encourages. Even from
the long title, the poet gets to raise his voice and go on instead of being
silent any longer! See what you think:

> *If the Kayaks Had Been Hung From the Rafters, I*
> *Could Have Driven My Truck Into the Barn, Parked*
> *and Loaded My Tools*

I didn't say, "Hey, you've owed me $250 for more than a year.
  You say
you're going to work it off, but then you never help me do
  anything."
I didn't say, "How about some respect? You're supposed to be
  honest
with me and helpful." When he stood us up for two dinner dates,
  I didn't
say, "Dope smoking is making your brain dead. You're becoming
an irresponsible jerk, self-centered and withdrawn. I didn't get on
  his case
about education, say I think he enjoys being ignorant, that he
  didn't even
graduate from high school, and if he doesn't respect me, imagine
what his son will say about him, a dope smoking redneck dad. I
  didn't give
him that last $50 for the power bill and I haven't heard from him
  since.

I did call the lawyer and get the house deal down on paper. I did make it
clear about what his obligations are, payments he must make etc. I did
tell him I thought smoking dope and whitewater kayaking down the river
don't mix. I did tell him it was time to think of Nya and the baby, life
insurance, that boring sort of responsible thing. I did tell him I have
expectations; he has obligations . . . time to be a grown-up daddy now.

Maybe this is how the message goes from father son to father son,
like a stick that tumbles down the rapids, like a kayak shell
that tumbles through white water, from level through level, down
the generations. And maybe a young man needs that kind
of turbulence, dumped out of his boat in white water.

Now that you've read the revision in long line form and felt the freedom in letting it all out, notice the line endings and beginnings. Every effort should be made to end lines with strong words and to begin as many lines as possible with stronger words than prepositions and articles.

After trying for stronger line endings and beginnings, look at the balance of the stanzas on the page: Do the stanzas and line lengths make a presence on the page that is welcoming and not unnecessarily unbalanced?

Often when adjusting line breaks for a visual pattern, you'll notice weaker lines where you are "telling" before "showing" in more vivid words. You may also notice flat spots where you are telling and not showing at all, or filling in narration for time clarity when the images already keep the reader posted. Later I will share Judy Tough's poem and revisions from the "I Saw You" exercise to illustrate this point.

THIS IS I

Gary Winans did the cluster on page 120 around the phrase "break day in Hakodate" to gather the details of his day during a business trip to Japan:

Then Gary wrote:

This is I who mixed my plate
　　of yellow scrambled eggs
　　with pencil lead skinny
　　strips of raw squid in soy sauce.
This is I who walked away
　　from circular tanks of hand-sized flatfish
　　flapping like small flags through the Siberian cold water.
This is I stripped naked with 5 other men
　　sitting in 42 C water watching steam
　　and snow flakes mix like our cultures.
This is I who was presented daikon seeds:
　　"Now you'll know my house in Seattle,
　　the one with the string of white daikon drying out front."
This is I who meditated
　　a darkened room in Hokkaido, me,
　　the red tip of incense glowing like
　　the moon crossed by snow.

I love this poem's details and the way we see the speaker getting used to a culture and its food, natural setting and customs. I like the difference between the flatfish in the cold water and the naked men mingling in hot water under a cold sky. I love the ending, which is so like Japanese lyric poetry, where the speaker and his environment are really one—meditating, he sees the tip of the burning incense as the moon in a snowy sky. The inside and outside are united, the small and the large, the up close and the faraway because in these moments and observations, the speaker has found his core that glows! The particular images given under each "This is I" sequence are to the point; short lines work to keep the poet and reader observant of the details and weighty importance of experiencing specifics, from eating new food, to doing the work the speaker is there to do, to being presented a gift, to participating in a social bathing, to having a private moment of impression. The indentations of the lines further emphasize the uniqueness and importance of each image until they overpower the "This is I" idea, fusing the I with his surroundings. Again, it's the emotional, design mind at work using the power of repetition to come to a new perception!

Bev Parsons wrote:

At Intensive Ten Day Music School

This is I who
crossed the road
today filled with expectation of the
first night in a motel.

This is I who
asked Steve if
he had a girlfriend
and he said,
"You don't really
want to know."

This is I who
played Schubert's Waltz
on the piano
for 25 people.

This is I who walked
across the bridge
marking the small stream
with a wind hurting my ears.

This is I who took a photo
of the wooden bridge
excluding Steve so as not
to raise any questions.

This is I who played
Muddy Waters on the cassette player
for everyone in the kitchen
hoping someone would move
and finally Helen did.

This is I who felt angry and
despaired at
a 3 month extension
to my boyfriend's
stay in India.

This is I who wanted to make
love with someone
anyone
I miss him
so much.

This is I
who wore
tinted sunglasses
so I could see things
in a different light.

Here we have short lines again, imitating the slowing down of
hesitancy, the stillness caused by being contemplative about behav-
ior, one's own and others, even as one is in motion with activity.
There are some places where the short lines make it seem as if the
speaker is so disappointed with the information, she can hardly bring
herself to say the words:

This is I who felt angry and
despaired at
a 3 month extension
to my boyfriend's
stay in India.

And there are other places where the short lines slow the reading
up enough for both the reader and poet to know how carefully they
are said, because they amount to a dangerous admission:

This is I who wanted to make
love with someone
anyone
I miss him
so much.

Keep a continuing sensitivity to line length when you revise, and
you will remain open to the meaning of your poem.

TONIGHT

New poet Diana Madaras wrote the following:

Tonight I Conquer My Computer

I sit before my computer contemplating poetry.
This gray buttoned alien with one huge eye is not my friend.
It beeps and grinds and even growls.
It flashes everything on its mind
across the screen but keeps secrets from me.

It talks sometimes but won't tell me
how to answer. It knows how to push
my buttons. I'm glad it can't get up and walk
around although I check on it from time to time
fearing it has learned a new skill overnight. I think
it may be smarter than me, too, but it hasn't figured out
the things I do when I have turned it off.

The speaker is in front of her computer; she sees it, hears it and
is frustrated by it. The details all come from this. The diction and

tone help us feel her frustration and the concern that machines we depend on can get the better of us. It's an alien with one eye and makes various beeps and grinds; it's capable, perhaps inadvertently, of power plays and keeping secrets. The fact that our speaker thinks it growls and may even get up and walk around give it monsterlike qualities it hasn't displayed but the speaker fears nonetheless.

Diana calls the poem "Tonight I Conquer My Computer," but it's not until the last line that we see how she will do that. By practicing this "tonight" exercise, she has the occasion to look at something seemingly poetically inconsequential and write why she is looking at the object. Only after stating the reasons does she create a title that explains why all of these reasons add up to something— way out of the computer's one-upmanship.

New poet Wanda Mawhinney wrote this from the "tonight" exercise:

Tonight's Full Moon

Thin transparent clouds
drape the moon with layers of gauze.

Dark mountains cut irregular shadows
against the crimson sky.

The full moon hangs
like a large eye
checking out the earth's movement,
casting pale light over the landscape.

Taillights weave like pairs of red eyes
along the winding road,
escapees from the city all
headed to the same place.

The moon smiles
and rises higher into the sky.

Are the escapees headed to view the moon? Are they, like lemmings, just leading a lifestyle unquestioningly? Can we tell from the poem? Does it matter if we can tell? To my sensibilities, all of these unanswered questions heighten the poem's mystery—the moon just smiles and rises higher into the sky as enigmatic as ever. It is usually distracting for a poet to personify something in the natural landscape, such as the moon, without making the subject silly. But I do not experience any distraction as I read Wanda's poem. So closely have her details (the gauzy layers; the shadows on the sky; the watchful eye of the moon; the fleeing, odd, red-eyed taillights) woven a spell, a full-moon spell, over me. I am a small child again—amazed.

WHEN I SAW YOU

The next three poems resulted from the "When I Saw You" exercise. The sensory details associated with seeing people in particular settings or on particular occasions carry the writers to perception and insight. In the first, the work started with Judy Tough's prosy portrait of her father when he was near death:

> When I visit you at your bidding, I enter the white walled bedroom in your assisted living apartment. Straight ahead next to the closet, hang four framed, matted, unbelievably young faces: you and Mom in sepia, Diana and I in color. Our family portraits preside over the lineup of medical servants: black and chrome wheelchair, steel walker, white plastic commode covered discreetly by a piece of printed tapestry, and a pulsing metal machine pushing oxygen through a clear tube into your waiting nose. As you hover on the edge of death, I sit on the edge of your single bed, feeling the stubborn tufts of the chenille bedspread. A folded red, white and blue afghan waits at your feet like a loyal dog. You smile. I lean over a frail, prone body dressed in red sweatpants and white tee shirt that says in bold red and blue letters: YOU CAN'T KEEP A GOOD KID DOWN. I kiss your scratchy, white whiskered cheek that smells of Burma Shave. The new home health aid hasn't perfected the art of shaving yet. "Hi, Honey." "Hi, Dad."

After looking at her description and feeling the certainty that this visit could stand for any of the last visits to her father, Judy used compression to create this version:

Last Visits

I saw you in the white walled bedroom
of your assisted living apartment
where next to the closet, four framed, matted,
unbelievably young faces hung:
you and Mom in sepia, Diana and I in color,
portraits presiding over a lineup of servants,
black and chrome wheelchair, steel walker, white
plastic commode covered by a piece of tapestry,
metal machine pulsing oxygen through a tube.

You hovered on the edge of death, an afghan
at your feet like a loyal dog. I sat on the edge
of your single bed, picking at stubborn
tufts of chenille on the spread. You smiled.
I leaned over you, frail and dressed in red
sweatpants. Your white t-shirt had bold blue
letters that said, "You can't keep a good kid down."
I kissed your scratchy, white whiskered
cheek and smelled your Burma Shave.

In the midst of death, the poet sees, in common details, the life—
a loyal dog, the Burma Shave, the portraits of the family in the room.
This is a poem about the difficulty of letting go ("stubborn tufts")
and it is told with trust in the details, including, of course, the irony
of the message on the T-shirt.

Meg Agnew was also inspired when closely observing someone
for whom she has strong feelings. Because this is someone she looks
at a lot, it helped Meg to start with the word "sometimes" so she
could focus on the small observations.

Sometimes When I Tuck You In

I sweep cinnamon strands of hair
from your face and my fingers
feel the smooth curve of your ear,
like the handle of a cup.
I inhale. I lean in and take a sip.

Diana Madaras also did the "When I Saw You" exercise. She had a strong childhood image of her mother raking leaves and forcing Diana to spend long hours at it when she really wanted to play:

Fall Funeral Pyre

I think of you raking on Sundays
near the river, the rake teeth scratching
through stones with the sound chalk
made on my teacher's blackboard.

You scooped up armfuls of leaves, buggy
and wet, put them on a fire where ashes
crackled and swirled in choking smoke.

I piled the wood you split, the stack never
neat enough. My friends spied on us
through the pines. I wanted to run.

I chewed the wet ties of my itchy
wool hat, rested whenever I could.
At night, I dreamt of leaves—marionettes
in wind, a ground with no color but snow.

I love this poem's understated evocation of some of the horrors of our childhood feelings. In a common fall scene, a daughter casts her mother as a witchlike woman capable of grabbing decay and bugs, trapping her daughter into labor that is never finished and never done well enough. Next, there is the evocation of another horror—embarrassment in knowing that school friends are watching. The speaker evokes her age seamlessly through details: the "sound chalk made" and the "wet ties of my itchy wool hat." The poem completes itself with a final image of "marionettes in wind" over a ground lacking all color but snow. Narratively speaking, snow would bring an end the girl's feelings of being a puppet on her mother's string; as an emotional image, it would blot out the distress of the situation.

Images convey emotional power by forming an occasion-specific constellation. In "When I Saw You Packing to Go Away" on page 98, Bev Parsons used a deceptively light hand to portray her concealed feelings upon her lover's leaving for a trip. They were hidden like the stuffed animal she had secretly buried in the suitcase. While that was a quiet action, it was rich in meaning. There was an important juxtaposition between the image of her heart going with her lover (the crushed bunny she hid in his suitcase), and the image of her holding the bag while he zipped it, a way of making them deal with his departure "rationally." The lines are short, making it take longer to read the poem, just as time seems when you are having last moments with someone. The images are sparse, too, like his packing and the good-bye they are trying to keep simple.

◆ ◆ ◆

In the next chapter, we will discuss the results of five more exercises: Three Days and Three Nights, Dreams, Mail, The Missing Eighty Miles and Dialogue. I hope you are working on your own poems from these exercises, too.

CHAPTER NINE

More on Using the Poet's Stance

The subjects of one's poems are the symbols of one's self or of one's selves.

—*Wallace Stevens*
from "Adagio"

In our outer lives, we are not consistent with our feelings and desires. Writing poems is a way of searching for an inner consistency that may or may not ultimately exist. When we write, we may feel as John Ciardi describes in *Dialogue With an Audience*:

> A poet thinks with his senses, his nerve endings, his whole body. He looks at his thought physically, and he looks from many directions at once. He *feels* what he thinks, and he feels it most in the act of making a poetic structure of it.

When we look over a poet's lifelong body of work, though, these many directions seem to organize around particular obsessions and themes. In the following results of the last five exercises from chapter five, you may be delighted to recognize individual poet's themes and obsessions. You may also be delighted to find them newly obsessed. One of the delights of writing from an assigned exercise is that poets get to write from occasions they might not have considered. They may use the occasion to return to the emotional territory of their usual obsessions, or to chart new territory. Either outcome is fine.

THREE DAYS AND THREE NIGHTS

Let's look at how Gary Winans created his "problem solution" in the exercise where he was to write part of the poem each night or day for three days. His first version below was recorded over four days. (I said to do three, but perhaps the first rule of poetry is to always customize the rules!) He didn't waste many words on section titles: Day 1, Day 2 and so on:

Day 1

i fill the bird feeder outside
with black sunflower seeds.
high white clouds, mostly blue sky
its supposed to be raining
my guess is 1 or 2 of my children are
still asleep at their house
will spring for the phone when it rings

i've had my espresso, black
i've fed the canary. he's singing.
i'm in sunlight on the floor
writing
lists form on my right on a clipboard
small plastic basketball hoop next to me
i need to fix before Adam comes over again

crackers, bits of crackers from last night when
Amanda and i watched TV until 9
they were all supposed to be here
but one was sick, preferred
his own bed, the other (Jeremy, the oldest)
went to a Sonics game

the radio: "I'm such a fool for you."
no, i'm such a fool, period, i think
why won't they just call me.

the bird is grooming in sunlight. a silhouette
if i squint.

i hope to drive my daughter to a party today
i hope they all eat dinner here tonight
this is MY weekend

i bought cod and broccoli and
potatoes. and grape koolaid.
the bird is singing. the sky is still
blue. it's supposed to rain.
i wish the phone would ring.

Day 2

one child stayed the night and
scrambled eggs for both of us while
i made toast and my coffee.
we watched the silly comedy on video
one more time
i let him sleep in my bed
his room is pretty empty:
dart board
couple of board games
a stuffed bear, some plastic Connects.

we wrestle, have lunch.

lying in bed, awake too early,
he's snoring next to me
i notice the screen in the window
is rattling. wind.
stop brain: no solutions.
i hear birds singing outside, the screen in the bedroom
window rattling in the wind, Adam snoring.

at age 10, they're buddies

Amanda stays till the video is over
wants to go home
makes a call before i take her,
and a neighbor meets her out front
when we arrive. she may be
only 1 of the few friends she told
about our separation.

the wind is still blowing, my guess 20-30
while Adam and his friend and i play
basketball at EC Hughes park.
i twirl them on the "merry-go-round"
until i'm queasy and sit on a bench.
the wind is in the southwest
they're still twirling.
i notice all the shadows in all of the footprints
in the sand play area and struggle
with myself for even considering windsurfing
i don't like myself then
i question how a selfish guy like me
could have stay married so long.

i give them each a dollar for a snack
at the corner store, which takes much debate
and weighing to spend, then i take them to the beach
to see check in out. they both complain
of belly aches and the wind.
we make a 3-stone totem
but i still feel stingy, confused.

Day 3

a work day. connected to my kids
by phone in the morning.

Adam and i start baseball practice
on a new clay field, dry
remarkably dry for march.
on the ride over, he is quiet, i think
he is mad at me; but its nerves he says.
we see a sliver of a waxing moon.
We reacquaint ourselves with last year's players
and 1/3 new faces.
the coach is in pain with a back injury
the other assistant coach says his voice
is in shape from coaching basketball.

i get paid today
my aliquot of my salary so buy food, gas, Adam
and me dinner.
Jeremy says please tell ALL my friends i don't
live there any more, he's tired of taking phone
messages—"very annoying," says the son
who always has plans when i would like him over
for dinner. he wants to pierce his eyebrow.
not with my money, i don't tell him.

phone calls, last minute papers and memos,
form updates, meeting scheduling keep me
from doing science today at work.
i don't talk by phone to my children—not unusual.

after practice, Adam says he forgot how much fun
baseball is, and he launches into a long monologue
about his prowess, history of great catches he's made—most of
    which i
didn't see, his extraordinary stats

and i remember how fun baseball with him
really is.

   I was excited by the poem I saw inside the lengthy notes. There
was definitely a theme of the speaker listening for his children; their
phone calls, their voices on the phone, their words during activities
and time together, and their underlying tone concerning whether
they still love him now that he and their mother have parted. In
proposing a revision, I suggested the title "Listening for My Children" since that is the emotional occasion that prompted his writing.
Most of the details and images are about his children and the feeling
tones he gets as he reads their voices and actions. When you read
the revision, notice what words were deleted because the information they held was better presented by a previous or following image.
For instance, espresso is black, so "black" is unnecessary.
   That the canary is singing in sunlight seems enough for Day 1.
Gary repeats the singing of the bird in this section, and I like the
way that makes the sunlight serve as a touchstone—a quick, almost

unnoticed reminder of the happiness and satisfaction he strives for
with his kids.

The lines "he wants to pierce his eyebrow / not with my money,
i don't tell him" will shift from Day 3 to Day 4 when life goes on
with its usual mixture of triumph, disagreement and busy moments.
By experiencing this continuation of family life, the problem of
whether the speaker is still loved by his children is transformed.

Listening for My Children
Day 1

I fill the bird feeder outside
with black sunflower seeds.
My guess is 1 or 2 of my children are
still asleep at their house.

I've had my espresso,
fed the canary singing
in sunlight. Lists form on my right
on a clipboard next to the basketball
hoop I need to fix before Adam comes again.

Bits of crackers from last night
where Amanda and I watched TV.
They were all supposed to be here
but Adam, sick, preferred
his own bed, and Jeremy
went to a Sonics game.

The radio: "I'm such a fool for you;"
I'm such a fool, period, I think.

I hope to drive my daughter to a party today
I hope they all eat dinner here tonight.
It is MY weekend
I bought cod and broccoli and
potatoes, grape koolaid and
the bird is singing.

Day 2

One child stayed the night and
scrambled eggs for both of us while
I made toast and my coffee.
We watched the silly comedy on video
I let him sleep in my bed;
his room is pretty empty:
dart board
couple of board games
a stuffed bear, some plastic Connects.

We'll wrestle, have lunch.

He's snoring next to me;
The screen in the window
is rattling. The wind is blowing 20-30.

Adam and his friend and I play
basketball at EC Hughs park.
I twirl them on the "merry-go-round"
until I'm queasy. I notice all the shadows
in all of the footprints in the sand play
area and struggle with myself for even
considering windsurfing.

How did a selfish guy like me
stay married so long?

I give them each a dollar for a snack
at the corner store, and getting it
takes much debate and weighing.
Then I take them to the beach;
they both complain of belly aches
and the wind. We make a 3-stone
totem but I still feel stingy and confused.

Day 3

Connected to my kids
by phone in the morning.

Adam and I start baseball
practice on a new clay field,
remarkably dry for March.
On the ride over, he is so quiet I think
he is mad at me; nerves, he says.
We see a sliver of waxing moon,
reacquaint ourselves with last year's players.

The coach is in pain with a back injury.

I buy Adam and me dinner.

Jeremy says please tell ALL my friends I don't
live there any more, he's tired of taking phone
messages—"very annoying," says the son
who always has plans when I would like him
over for dinner.

     Day 4

I hear from my kids. Adam forgot how
much fun baseball is, the history
of great catches he's made. Jeremy
wants to pierce his eyebrow—
not with my money, I don't tell him.

Phone calls, last minute papers and memos,
form updates, meeting scheduling.
It was supposed to be raining
but it's high white clouds and mostly blue sky.

DREAMS

Notice in the following exercise results how the speaker evokes the
chilling contrasts between our dream world and our waking world.
Recounting a dream in a poem that is ultimately for an audience, if
only an audience of one, forces the issue of more fully living the
experience the dream has brought.

    Diana Madaras, who is a ready rememberer of her dreams, did
this exercise in almost Dr. Seuss-like rhythm and sound pattern:

A Dream in a Tree

I sat in the V of a tree with no leaves
and only one branch and a trunk
too wide to embrace. I gazed to the sea
holding my cat, protecting his life
from the terrible heights that we faced.
I trembled with fear of falling from high,
and I clutched to the trunk and the cat.

I called to a friend who passed
right below, said, "Fetch me
a ladder and fast." He climbed up
the tree to resuscitate me. It felt
like a near heart attack. When I jumped
to the top of the ladder he brought, I saw
I was only two feet up the tree.

I tell you this dream and it sounds
like a joke, but I awoke in a sweat
and my palms were all wet and my heart
beat like hooves on a track.

Perhaps I can't really climb to great
heights, though I think that I would
to protect your cat life. I tell you this
and you just sleep at the foot of my bed
while I worked so hard through the night!

Who hasn't awakened from a dream to find our household sleeping or going about their business as if the experience in our dream never happened—as if we, too, should just forget it!

Wanda Mawhinney, neuromuscular therapist, wrote this dream poem:

The Woman With No Shoulder Blade

In my dream a woman with dishwater hair
and faded cotton print dress directs
pedestrians across a street.

Her hair, dress and skin have the same
tone, like dry desert dirt in the middle of summer.

Her eyes are pale as wedgewood
plates staring at us as she waves us across the street.
People obey, cattle driven into a pen. When I turn,
her back is toward me and I see she has no left
shoulder blade, just area flat and scarred like a mastectomy.

Another night sweat jerked me out of dreams.
I throw covers off my steaming body,
tell you that images return.

This becomes a poem about a haunting. Our speaker does not
pretend to know who her dream visitor may be, but she knows the
visit is linked with night sweats and she can't shuck it off.

Liz Gamberg wrote the following dream as if she were telling it
to the little boy she'd dreamt about:

About Jonah, From a Dream

I hold this picture close
   when I am at cliff's edge,
   when the door I thought
   was closed, opens.

I carry this dream of you
   jumping from a high place
   landing easily on your feet
   right side up, as if you were
   your own parachute.

The last time I had dinner
   with you and your sister
   every cell in your thick earthy body
   from your eyebrows to your toes
   was in the appleseed prayer
   we sang in thanks for the food
   we were about to eat.
      the earth is good to me

and so I thank the earth
for giving me the things I need
the sun and the rain and the appleseed
the earth is good to me.

In addressing the little boy, Liz has the same undercurrent to her words as the writers above who kept the fact that they were addressing someone a secret till the third or fourth stanzas. She still juxtaposes what she has learned from her dream with what she saw and experienced—the value of belief, of full-bodied participation in life.

MAIL
Voice Mail

Esther Altshul Helfgott did the voice mail exercise in a fanciful way. Her daily greetings have personality and presence. They challenge the caller to have them, too!

> this is Monday, not the day i wash my clothes though but i should, you know. mother did. she used to wash with a scrub board, singing all the while. imagine, down on her knees in front of the old white tub with the funny legs making it stand six inches above the floor. dirt got underneath and we had to sweep it out/off the blotchy linoleum whose corners turned up at the end. this was the 1950s and most of the time the laundry man picked up our clothes to wash and we hung them around the same tub to dry. if our underwear didn't dry by the time we went to school the next morning, we laid them out flat on the oven door. anyway, that's what i'm thinking on this Mon. what are you thinking? leave a message after the beep.

> Tuesday is for washing the dog, but i'm too busy reading Marie Cardinal's words to wash the dog. are you washing your dog? do you have one? have you read Marie Cardinal? how come you're calling anyway? sing me a song, if you will. i shan't laugh, shall you?

> what are you doing today? i'll answer your message when i finish my book/ Love, esther

Wednesday is for taking a rest so why are you bothering me with your call? don't you ever rest during the day, cuddle up with pencils and paper and crayons or a fun magazine when you've finished your book? go way, come back some other day, unless of course you just must leave a message then you can do so after the beep. you have three minutes. get ready, get set, go!

Thursday is fool's day so leave me a fool. after the beep.

Friday is on the way to the weekend day when all day long the next day . . . oh, you wish you knew. leave us a message and a wish too. after the beep.

These greetings have the sound of free associational thinking. By allowing herself that freedom, Esther included things she may not have in a more serious vein. Now that she has committed these free associational thoughts to days of the week, a voice becomes clear— that of an educated, friendly, uninhibited but private woman who inspires me to leave her an entertaining message, and who I certainly hope will get back to me!

When I looked and listened into this exercise result with my poem sculptor eyes and ears, I proposed tightening the writing to heighten the voice that was emerging. For instance, I thought the first day's greeting might read:

Monday

This is the weekday my mother washed our clothes
with a scrub board, singing all the while.
If our underwear wasn't dry when we dressed
for school the next morning, we laid it out flat
on the oven door. That's what I'm thinking on this
Monday morning. What are you thinking? Leave
a message after the beep.

Esther felt the presence of her mother was best evoked by including her sound in the stanza. She titled the new version with a title that speaks to the truth in the poem: If you want to reach the very real self who speaks in these lines, you'll have to accept her on her own terms and give her the conversation, information and genuine qualities she demonstrates herself!

Here's a later version:

Reaching Me: Voice Mail Instructions
Monday

This is the weekday my mother washed our clothes
with a scrub board, singing all the while,
"On the line, on the line, all my little children's
clothes are on the line." If our underwear wasn't
dry when we dressed for school the next morning,
we laid it out flat on the oven door, the three of us
competing for space as always. That's what I'm
thinking on this Monday morning. What are you thinking?
Leave a message after the beep.

Tuesday

This day's for washing the dog but I'm
too busy reading Marie Cardinal's words
to wash the dog. Are you washing your dog?
Do you have? Have you read Marie Cardinal?
How come you're calling anyway? Sing me a song,
if you will. I shan't laugh, shall you?
What are you doing today? I'll answer your message
when I finish my book.

Wednesday

A day for taking a rest so why are you
bothering me with your call? Don't you ever
rest during the day, cuddle up with pencils
and paper and crayons, a fun magazine when you've
finished your book? Go away, come back some other
day, unless of course you just must leave a message
then you can do so after the beep. You have three minutes,
get ready, get set, go!

Thursday

It's a fool's day so leave me a fool.
After the beep.

Friday

I'm on my way to the weekend days when all day long
the next day, oh, you wish you knew. Leave us
a message and a wish, too. After the beep.

Then Esther wrote another revision and presented this one at a
reading to enthusiastic response. Compare it to the one above; see
what you miss from the old version and what you like from this
newest one. Decide which version you would prefer if you were an
editor of a literary magazine. Support your decision with a discussion
similar to ones I've shared for student poems. Remember to think
about the sounds, line breaks, tone, specificity of images and how
the images build so the poem can weigh more at the bottom than
at the top.

Reaching Me: Voice Mail Instructions
Monday

On this weekday, Mother washed our clothes,
got down on her knees in front of the tub
and scrubbed. In anticipation of the job to follow,
she sang: "On the line, on the line,
all my little children's clothes are on the line.
If you want to get 'em clean,
you have to rub and scrub,
and hang those clothes out to dry."
Leave me a message, after the beep.
Beeeep.

Tuesday

This is the day to wash the dog,
but I'm too busy reading Marie Cardinal
to wash the dog. Do you have a dog?

Have you read Cardinal?
How come you're calling anyway?
Sing me a message, won't you?
I shan't laugh;
will you, after the beep?
Beep.

Wednesday

My writing needs a rest. So do I.
So why are you bothering me with your call?
Don't you ever rest during the day, cuddle up
with pencils, crayons and paint? A fun little
'zine? Go away. Call again another day.
Unless, you just *must* leave me a message.
Then, of course, you can—after the beep.
You'll only have three minutes though.
So get ready, get set. Go!

Thursday

It's a fool's day, so leave me a fool.
After the beep. Beep.

Friday

I'm off for the weekend, but only after
I finish the bibliography for the paper I'm writing.
So I can't possibly answer your call right now.
I have to get through. Oh, if I only knew
what tomorrow will bring. I think I do.
I hope I do. Do you, for you? Tell me a tale,
specific to you. After the beep. Beep.

Postcards

Sometimes when we direct our words to another, at least in our imaginations, we write from a place deep in ourselves. Richard Hugo wrote himself out of a writer's block with letter poems addressed to poets he knew, to poets whose work he appreciated, and to significant friends. The poems eventually became a collection called *31 Letters and 13 Dreams.*

Diana Madaras was inspired to do the postcard exercise while on vacation in the Caribbean. She felt her sister's absence.

Postcard From Bahamia

Dear Sister:

I miss you on our island vacation
this year. Ten years ago I couldn't say
that; I could hardly speak your name.

Rusty memories of childhood tricks
and rejections like kicks from a blackbelt,
betrayals putting Brutus to shame
kept us circling—hunter and prey.

It took tropical laser rays to cut away
the cold places in my heart. The night tides
licked our wounds and salt air eroded tall
walls of junk. It softened me
to laugh full out with you.

Here we learned a language
we could talk. Come back to our island
with me next year, seek starfish in the rain.

I'm fond of the way the postcard message uses the imagery of the tropics—sun rays and night tides—to evoke the process of the emotional change the speaker acknowledges. I very much like the line, "Here we learned a language / we could talk." It is rhythmic and easy to say, but difficult to do so without feeling the foot of its meter in your own heart. "Starfish in the rain" seems an appropriate melding in image form of the sea life of the Caribbean and the emotional life of sisters who have too long been distant.

Next are a series of postcard messages Liz Gamberg wrote and made into one poem with her title:

Postcards About Hope

Dear Janet—I liked talking to you last night about e-mail/voice
mail and that feeling of   being beholden to it because maybe
    there
will be a message this time I check. Maybe   someone tried to
    call
while I was on the phone. Taps into the hopeful part of us. You
likened it to gambling.
    I loved seeing the new chapel at SU with you—beeswax-lined
    walls
in the alcove the   LB designed, with the madrona tree. Gold leaf
where limbs had been chopped off.   The quote by Ignatius about
    the
lion's teeth. Celtic prayer that you thought was zen   like. And
the quote by St. Catherine of Siena about god being a waiter.
    Different
colors of light coming through the small odd opening and windows,
    and
the 3 jars of oils   by the baptismal font. Felt good and
peaceful to be in there and to know the place is   there.
Reminded me that when I was at Vassar, I used to go to chapel
    some
sundays   just to be in a peaceful place sacred to some—for
the form even if not for the content.   Did you ever notice how
    close
in spelling the words "sacred" and "scared" are?
love liz

Dear Anne Lamott—I loved hearing you last night. Your sage
    humor and
honesty fed me. It was a luscious meal. You said publishing early
drafts is like showing people your thighs—yeah, they really do
    have
dimples. You said you were a black-belt people pleaser when you
    were a kid—and
"how thin the membrane between order and chaos." And your
    editor was
good at finding connective tissue between pieces in your books—
    and 85%

of good writing is from taking the therapist out of it.
If what you publish is 3 to 4 rings out from the bull's eye, then
    what's
IN the bull's eye?
How alive am I willing to be, you asked all of us?
I'm not sure.
But thanks for looking into the abyss and writing about it.
liz

Dear Liza—Thanks for coming to the studio last night. Just at the
right time, as I was pissed and feeling sorry for myself because I
couldn't find what I needed to fire the kiln. Whisking me off to
    dinner
was the perfect thing. loved talking to you about LB's part of the
    new
chapel at SU—how you talked to her about it—and how you could
    feel
its construction vs. it just being an art piece. And she wanted to
evoke the feeling of the people traveling across lands and
    constructing
sacred sites wherever they ended up.
And thank you for telling me that when you're intimidated by
    someone,
you just imagine them in their underwear.
love liz

Dear morning—Some mornings if I drive by the zoo on my way
    to work, I
notice that the color of one of the green lights at 50th & Phinney is
slightly different than the green of the one next to it. I like when I
notice that because it means I am paying attention.
This morning, I sit in bed propped up against pillows, skylights
    open,
no wind, very still all of a sudden. The red and yellow flag by the
Buddhist temple a few blocks away is barely waving in the breeze.
    Looks
like it's in slow motion. I watch it through spaces in the slats of
    the
blinds which separates everything into separate frames.
love, Liz

I admire how this string of messages moves through the world of friends and activities, sights and lectures, until the last message when the insights are inward and self-initiated. Then they are directed to privateness, to the morning as a silent friend who comes bearing nonverbal gifts! The poem is prosy, but I can't think of words or phrases that could come out without diminishing the voice of the speaker, who builds from an appreciation of the words and wisdom of others to the ability to find and honor her own hope. Since I am unwilling to part with words here, I believe this is a prose poem. A prose poem is defined by William Packard in *The Poet's Dictionary: A Handbook of Prosody and Poetic Devices* as: "Poetry having a high incidence of sight and sound and voice devices, but with no formal line arrangements; prose poems resemble loose paragraphs and are sometimes called 'vignettes.' " I reread Liz's messages and note that the poetry of the first message is in the details she tells the person she is thanking. She has filtered what each has said and constructed from the remembered words an apparatus for hope. The message to morning has the densest images—the view out the window of a flag in slow motion, the blinds separating things into their own spaces. These images work to build an inner landscape of slowing down, paying attention, being present. Of what else is hope made?

Gary Winans also did a postcard poem:

> *On Finding the O'Keefe Postcard of*
> *Morning Glories I'd Meant to Mail to Dad,*
> *Was Hoping to Mail This Spring*
> For Russell Winans, 1915 to 1996
>
> I remember your spring ritual
>   at the kitchen table
>   with white ceramic bowl of water,
>   jackknife, cutting board
>   you had made at Kiwanis
>   with the whittled remnant of a decal
>   at the top; your ringless meticulous
>   fingers making diamond-cutter nicks
>   on the millet-colored seeds hard as rocks
>   from Burpee Seed called Heavenly Blue
>   you'd soak overnight before planting.

I showed my kids the ceremony
> tried a mix of colors, pinks, scarlets, creams
> with and without creamy veins,
> from Johnnies of Maine.
> I tried a jackknife; I tried sandpaper.

It's too late to share this on the postcard—you'd have
doubted the O'Keefe colors anyway not Heavenly Blue.
It's too late to tell you
> I soak seeds in a wet paper towel
> and plant the sprouts to form a small
> squadron of green butterflies along the wood
> strip pegged with penny nails, to tell you how
> they wait for the cord I'll string to help them fly.

This poem moves me. I admire the way the speaker takes the time to tell his father's simple seed-starting ritual, to tell the way he showed his kids the ritual, and the way he plants in spring. What the speaker's father planted imprinted on the mind and the heart of his son. There is, of course, a measure of the eternal in the son's sharing this with his own children. This poem was prompted by a small occasion—finding the postcard he planned on sending as his own ritual to honor his father. And it turns quite simply into a big occasion, that of eulogizing his father.

Book Rate

Marilyn Meyer set out to do the book rate variation of this exercise. But instead of buying her friend a book, she bought her a bracelet and tucked this note into the package:

Note Tucked Into a Birthday Present

Happy, Happy Birthday, Karen.
What does a thin, linked silver bracelet
with six polished stones have to do with turning fifty?
I bought two of them at the Vancouver
Folk Festival last weekend. I wore mine
and smiled, thought of you opening
this package, thought of the way your brown
eyes, dark and translucent like these stones,

would narrow slightly, as you unfold the gauze
wrapping, how you would smile when you discover
this poem between the layers, how there would be love
and humor and just a few wrinkles underneath.

At the festival I stood in line to use the row of sani-cans.
Way over to the left music from Mali billowed
from Stage Five like curling smoke from a hookah.
Behind me two women in their sixties stood together
in the warm July sun. The younger, her belly
round like a Ukrainian grandmother's, wore a long loose
dress and floppy straw hat. The elder, her white hair
wrapped in coils above her head, had lifted the front
hem of her long Indian gauze skirt, tucked it into the waist.

Gracefully she gyrated to the African rhythms,
arms extended, palms raised, hips shaking,
belly swaying, breasts bobbing from their halter hammock.
They told me they were sisters from Seattle, the dancer
studying belly dancing, tango, rumba and swing.
The younger had just begun her first corporate job—as a midwife.
"Time for someone else to pay the health insurance,"
she said dabbling sun screen on her sister's golden shoulders.

That night in the woods someone shined a flashlight
at our tent around midnight, just as I
reached orgasm, just as I moaned, sighed in passion.
Mark peeked out of the tent, said he saw the mother
from the neighboring tent, that she must have
heard something in the night and "maybe it was you."

This morning we saw her at a restaurant in town. She turned
away. Her husband approached Mark, made small talk
about ferries, then smiled at me and shook my hand.

Let me tell you about being fifty:
It's a few more wrinkles, gray hair at your crowns,
a rounder belly, wider hips and skinnier legs,
but, oh, the freedom to enjoy them.

It is fun to get so involved in the people at the folk festival and the campground that for awhile you forget this is a note accompanying a present to a friend who is turning fifty. By the poem's end, the bigger present has become not only the poet's expression of feeling for her friend, but for all women, herself included, as they age and enjoy who they are! "Welcome to our wonderful community," the note is saying, and because of its metaphors about wrinkles in the tissue paper, the face and the friendship, it means, "I'm glad we've seen each other through to this transition."

THE MISSING EIGHTY MILES

The following two poems were written by students who thought of a particular stretch of road and let themselves entertain the experience of being on it. Wanda Mawhinney wrote:

The Next 80 Miles

Through the sheets of rain
I almost miss the green sign
    BOISE
    80 MILES

I squirm, shift my body in reluctant preparation.

The arc cleared by the wipers
immediately disappears from the windshield.

click, click, scoop, scoop

The rhythm makes my eyes heavy,
blurred lights stare at me,
wet tires scream, "She's dead."

You didn't come soon enough.
You didn't come when I called.
You weren't here when I needed you

"She needed you!"

I didn't think she meant so soon
I didn't want to hear her words
I thought I had time

BOISE
40 MILES

Click, click, scoop, scoop

"She's dead,"
You didn't come soon enough!

click, click, scoop, scoop

Wanda has used the eighty-mile exercise as an opportunity to incorporate one of the sound tools discussed in chapter four. She also did the dialogue exercise in combination with the eighty-mile idea. Both the onomatopoeia and the direct speech serve her evocation of the physical and emotional occasion that inspired the poem. The line "wet tires scream, 'She's dead,' " imitates the sound of a car screeching to a halt. Then Wanda continues: *"You didn't come soon enough. / You didn't come when I called. / You weren't there when I needed you."* These lines simulate the rhythm of tires on a wet road. Incorporated into the poet's ability to continue driving is her articulation of what she fears most—not the death but the accusations when she arrives. There is definitely, even in this extreme situation, a humor evolving in the last line: "click, click, scoop, scoop." These sounds end the poem like a statement summing things up: the click, click of the wagging tongues, and the scoop, scoop of the speaker's ready shovel against the inevitable shit she's in or the dirt to be moved for a burial.

As for dialogue, the speaker has woven in and played against three voices: the road's accusations in "She's dead," the accuser's voice in italics (most likely a relative) and the speaker's voice in the eighth stanza. The words, sounds, setting and repetitions tell a big story in a short space—we feel we are journeying under external, internal, archetypal and physiological pressure!

Gary Winans also did this exercise. He used the miles around the place where he grew up and where his father was born. By fully

imagining them and their landmarks, Gary has attributed some of
who he is to the source—the life of his father:

Where My Father Was Born, Battle Creek River

Let's start at the Mill House downtown Battle Creek,
at the corner of Michigan Avenue and Capital.
Where the display of crashing water is endlessly demonstrating
falling water's power to make flour, cut wood
you smell breakfast cereal from Kellogg's' ovens when the wind
is from the east

Let's follow the river north through
Verona along River Road, through Verona where Dad was raised
through Bailey Park where we learned baseball,
walked to the 4th of July carnival for rides, cotton candy,
dusty shoes.
You can drive past a cattail rich waterway;
it smells green. Red-winged blackbirds
scold as you approach the banks.
Uncle Hi lived near a sharp bend where the water was green, slack;
he pumped it into his garden, grew cabbages Dad never tried.
"Too wormy without chemicals," he said.

There's a flood plain before it enters Wanadoger neighborhood;
the W. Creek winds through this n-hood
used for skating in the winter, by the Simpsons, Wests, Martins.
Park at the railing of Pennfield Road before the mosquitoes
    thicken
the air. Mr. Worthington, butch cut, large patient hands, still
leads students through the flood plain
upriver teaching skunk
cabbage and trillium.
We need to go north now on M-66 past the sharp curve
at the cemetery by White Rabbit Road and head towards Bellevue

past Bus Morris's place with the barn and swimming pool, past
    Rick

Proos's house off the road. Judy and Jim Treadwell lived right next
    to
the road.
Or veer left on M-66 and head to Nashville where Dad was born
near the river he said
a town of tall wooden store fronts
with bric-a-brac edges and broad windows
white court house, 2 gas stations, a feed store with wooden loading
dock
littered with straw and grain and Dairy Queen, the river park
with maples where they have a syrup festival, a cemetery, a 9-hole
golf course on converted pasture, and then the flat farm land of
    SE
Michigan
where counting barns is still a good game
doing M-66 north
and don't miss the round barn on the east side,
getting close now to the source.

Many of the lines in this poem are long and don't differ much
from travelogue speech, but it is definitely arranged in line breaks
and they do make the voice more intense. Amidst the long, folksy
lines, the voice sometimes comes down in strokes of one- or two-
word lines: Michigan, dock, the road. An intensity accompanies this
as the voice stops after longer lines, and this intensity is born of an
echoing of midwestern-clipped, I'm-not-a-man-of-many-words kind
of speech. This is an embodied kind of remembering and Gary pulls
from himself an experience of a "fatherland," of growing up in a
place, of coming from a source, as he travels to the source of the
river.

DIALOGUE

Following the dialogue exercise, Judy Tough wrote these poignant
sentences her father spoke:

You know, I only have 15% of my heart left.
My heart will never get better; there is no way they can fix it.
The only way I'd get better is to get a new one, but get in line!
I only have more trips to the hospital and more illness to look
    forward to.

I suggested Judy title her poem in progress. From there she could either choose the block method in which these four lines come first and she responds in a second stanza, or the alternating method where each of the four lines introduces a stanza. I am in favor of the alternating method here because each of her father's lines is a down line. It would be interesting to see what response each down line triggers in the speaker. First she might retort in her thoughts that the 15 percent left is important—which part of the heart remains so close to the end? What does she feel thinking about her father being this way? Then she might free associate with times in her life when she felt there was no hope, when she said it could never be done. When the father says, " . . . but get in line," Judy might associate with lines she waited in with her dad or without his knowledge or despite his opinion. Finally, in response to the last line, she might offer him smaller, up-close things to look forward to each day, or she might meditate on what she hopes for herself in the days near his or her own death. These lines copied from heard speech are jumping-off places, diving boards for poetic inquiry.

Here is what Judy wrote:

> *Meditations on Words My Dying Father Spoke*
> With gratitude to James Merrill after reading his
> poems in *A Scattering of Salts* and Wendell Berry
> for his poem "The Larger Circle."

"My heart will never get better; there is no way they can fix it."
Unrequited dream of the Fountain of Youth and Perpetual Health!
Now bereavement, fury, grief. Glimmerings found in maternal/
    paternal
genes and DNA; all were present at your creation.
Life, without its consort Death, would be hell. Nature,
by definition, is sane.

"You know, I only have 15% of my heart left."
I give thanks! Four score years you have lived. Was the missing
muscle used up in sweat, family, friends, devotion to church,
boiled away in yesteryear's youth? No matter! Distilled,
what remains warms itself at the hearth glowing in Mom's eyes.

"The only way I'd get better is to get a new one, but get in line!"
Queue up, this is an Express Line. Fifteen items or less!
Join hands with those who have gone before us and those who
    follow.
Enter the Final Dance, the circle of all creatures passing in and
    out of Life,
Moving to a music so vast and whose rhythm we've just begun to
    know.

"I only have more trips to the hospital and more illness to look
    forward to."
What trips has your soul taken? I never listened if you spoke of this.
As your soul became a self did it step in and out of dark woods?
Were you a stranger to fire; were you not scarred?
Life has held you, may it's arms mottled with wisdom embrace
and comfort you while on the way.

Judy said she never could have written the poem without having
read and found solace from the work of Wendell Berry and James
Merrill, whose words influenced her meditation. Poets acknowledge
direct influences from whom they have borrowed, or sometimes
even stolen, with epigraphs under the title. Reading other poets is
always a good way to invite our own poetry to enter us.

Liz Gamberg composed this poem:

> *something resulting from a dialog*
> *I had in the Methow Valley*

in the house filled with families of four
I sit down at the table with the colored
pencils and pastels, more than colors
of the rainbow, each in the slots of the box
where they belong. Alexandra, age 7,
sits across from me. we introduce ourselves;
her paper is filled with color and I decide
which pastel to choose first.

"do you have a kid here?" *no.* "do you have kids
who ride the bus to Coho Elementary?"
no. why? are there kids on your bus
who look like me? "uh huh. do you wish you

had kids?" *sort of. but it probably won't happen.*
"well, they aren't so bad once you get to know them."

I admire this poem for the way it carries a surprise and jolts us, along with the speaker, out of one world and into another. Adults may mourn not having children or decide they are pleased not to have had them, but children can only be on the side of having them. By using very simple language and little capitalization, this poem brings the rationalizing, choice-making world of the adults head to head with the belief system of children, which is grounded in what is and what they are.

CONTINUING TO FIND MATERIAL ON YOUR OWN

We have discussed the development of poems from exercises designed to make writers use common-life images in structures that throw them "against the silence," where they will then arrive at insight. The insight that arises from experience as it is relived in imagery is the very heart of poems. Without this insight, a poem would only be a pulse with no heart—a weird, disembodied energy that couldn't come down to earth and course through our veins. Choosing events from everyday life but endowing them with mystery guarantees the "calling down" and grounding that poets must accomplish to express the inexpressible, to make tangible the intangible, to see the eternal and timeless in the everyday.

To continue writing poems, redo any of the exercises in this book using fresh images. You will get new results. You can also invent your own strategies for juxtaposing events against the silence. Here are two examples:

1. Invite someone to do something specific and name a poem after that invitation, for example, "Inviting My Daughter to Read Cinderella With Me."

2. Address your wishful self to something that can't tangibly grant your wish and name a poem after that request, for instance, "Asking the Oleander Leaves to Help Me Understand Poison."

Just keep paying attention to overlooked or unusual opportunities for people and things to speak to you or for you.

A NOTE ON THE PROCESS OF REVISION

When you have some words down on paper that are either from an exercise or a start to a poem, develop them into a poem by paying attention to the words in the way I have when discussing the work of poets in this book.

First, let yourself have some time away from the words. Turn your attention to something else for a few hours, although a day or two is even better. Give yourself enough time to feel detached from the joy that you were writing a poem to clearly see what you have put on the page. Sometimes mailing a copy of the work to yourself helps give you this time and distance.

Next, read your work for words that are tangible. Where have you written images and details that can be touched, smelled, tasted, heard or seen? You might even want to list these words to reinforce their value.

Next, read for words that are summarizing—joy, sorrow, happiness, beauty, rushed, depressed—any words that tell about a state of being or an emotion without sharing a specific experience from which one would get those feelings or ideas.

Go back into your words and supply details that appeal to and are known through the five senses. Look for any cliches that have crept into your work and replace them with original detail and ways of saying what you are wanting to evoke. Use metaphor if you can and be sure your metaphorical thinking is creating a unified emotional landscape.

Make sure your words are consistent with the tone of the emotion. Be wary of words that are in high diction: Is your left-brain, ego-based writing self taking over and tuning out the shy, design-minded, evocative, right-brain writing self? Also, be wary of words that are too low in diction and make the reader giggle when that is not appropriate. A friend of mine once wrote a love poem and put the word "jammies" in it, which was too colloquial and childlike for the mature sexual feelings in the poem.

Check out other kinds of sound. Are there rhythms that are distracting because they call attention to themselves and change the emotional response of the reader? For instance, your poem might be conversational in tone and suddenly have a strong resemblance to the sound of a hymn or the "Pledge of Allegiance." If this happens, try to think about why that sound crept in. Are you wanting to make a reference or association to something inherent in the church scene or to your school or scouting years? If so, write about those experiences with details—the where, when, what, who, how stuff:

> Mrs. Hemmerly sat on the edge of her teacher's desk
> facing the class, her legs crossed at the knees.
> Where she held the chalk in her fingers, I could
> almost see cigarette smoke and a sleek black holder.

Unify what you are writing about; make the occasion in a particular time and place. You may move around in your thoughts and associations, but the reader should always be able to figure out where you are speaking from and upon what occasion you began speaking. Put this occasion or place in the title to help you unify what you have written.

Look at your line breaks and make sure that as often as possible, they begin and end with strong words rather than prepositions, articles or conjunctions.

Look for words that are doing the work other words are already doing better, and delete them. Remember, a poem is a concentrated form of language.

Try your poem out on trusted listeners. Get their response in the three stages I will discuss in chapter ten. Briefly, this amounts to first asking them what words and phrases they remember. This will give you an idea of the impact of your words. Then ask them what their overall feeling is, for instance, do they feel joy, sadness, despair, awe, gratitude, loneliness or yearning? Then ask them what words, sounds and phrases go against the feeling they think the poem wants to evoke. Finally, ask them if they need more information or insight. They can tell you this in the form of questions or statements: "I don't know where the I is when the poem is being read," or "Where is the I who is speaking to me?"

Poetry writing workshops are the best help in revising poems and bringing them fully into being. In the next chapter and appendices, I include information on finding groups in your area. I also include resources for finding professionally facilitated poetry writing workshops.

No matter how long you continue writing poetry, you may always wish for sensitive response. I still work with a writing group once a month. With one old-time poet friend who now lives a distance away, I use the mail to be sure I get a trusted response to my beginnings.

◆ ◆ ◆

Now let's discuss these groups and more of the tasks of the poet— readings, literary activities, building collections and publishing them.

CHAPTER TEN

Continuing On

. . . make this the year to revive your dreams, whatever they may be—publication to Pulitzers—and go about the business of understanding how to achieve them.
—Michael J. Bugeja
1993 Poet's Market

In addition to creating and shaping their poems, poets are usually concerned with continuing their study of poets and poetry, and eventually with reading their poems in public forums, publishing their poems and participating in the creation of poetry events. These aspects of the poet's life require time, periodic seclusion, resource information and the companionship and ideas of nearby poets.

When I began studying poetry writing at the University of Washington, professor Nelson Bentley distributed dittoed lists of journals to which he thought we should submit our work. Other professors also told us about literary magazines they or their colleagues edited. Under Professor Bentley's coordination, the University of Washington's Castillia Poetry Readings were held three times a week, and former and current UW poets read their work before an interested and enthusiastic audience. Eventually a fine, independent bookstore, Elliott Bay Books, opened and drew national poets there to read from their books (not that many of the former UW poets weren't nationally recognized themselves!). Additionally, a group called Red Sky Poetry Theater began as an alternative, nonacademy-based, grassroots, multicultural venue for local poets. The annual Labor Day Weekend Bumbershoot Arts festival expanded literary programming to include readings, festival publications and a small press bookfair, which helped us learn more about poetry and poets in our region and the country. Now, twenty plus years later, we have an annual NW Bookfest attracting regional and national publishers, editors and writers; creative writing departments in several area colleges and universities; and more bookstore and community center readings and poetry publications than it is possible to attend or read in any given week. From the days when I first began to find out about the literary scene until now, I have amassed much helpful information. To present it to you, I have divided the information into five helpful categories: (1) studying the craft—where to find teaching materials and resources including time and seclusion; (2) forming a writers' group—how to do this and what to do at such a group; (3) publishing your poems—how to go about sending work out; (4) building a collection—how to figure out readiness to submit a manuscript for a chapbook or poetry book publication; and (5) participating in literary events—where to find them and how to have a role in them.

Information is a lot easier to come by these days, but you can probably still use a guide. If what follows seems like too much information and recommended activity when your focus is writing poems, remember that you decide how much you want to take on, how rapidly, and how often. At least the information is here, all in one place, until you need it!

STUDYING THE CRAFT

The study of poetry is beginning to have a higher public profile since Bill Moyer's efforts with programs on National Public Television, such as his five-part series *The United States of Poetry*. From this series, a coffee-table book of poems and photographs was published (Harry N. Abrams) and a condensed soundtrack album was released (Almighty/Mercury). But the less-glossy, lower-profile publications and organizations are where the most information is available.

This book's appendices include an annotated bibliography of books on writing poetry, books of writings by poets on poetry, books on creativity, anthologies of poetry and collections by individual poets. I have listed the particular poets in my library. In addition to studying these books, you can pursue your study with the following resources.

Major Poetry Book Series Award Publications

Several organizations award book publication to poets each year in conjunction with literary presses. Some of the many worth looking for are: Beacon Press/Barnard New Women Poets Prize; Yale Younger Poet Series; Walt Whitman Award from the Academy of American Poets; the New Rivers Press Minnesota New Voices Project Winner; the Western Book Awards winner in poetry; the National Book Awards in Poetry; the National Poetry Series winners; and the AWP Award Series publications in poetry. If your local booksellers can't find these, you can probably locate copies by calling the poetry-only bookstores listed later.

Major Literary Reviews and Magazines

You should become acquainted with the biggest names in literary small press publishing. These literary reviews can usually be found at your library, fine magazine newsstands or a good bookstore's magazine rack. You can see ads for them in many of the poetry resource magazines and newsletters listed in this chapter. A few of the notable titles follow.

The American Poetry Review, 1721 Walnut St., Philadelphia, PA 19103-5236, (215) 496-0431. According to *The Poet's Market*, Writer's Digest Books' respected guide to poetry resources and publications, this review is "a major resource for opinion, reviews, theory, news and ads pertaining to poetry," and "may be the most widely circulated and best-known periodical devoted to poetry in the world."

The Boston Review, Boston Review Department of Political Science, E53-407, Massachusetts Institute of Technology, Cambridge, MA 02139, (617) 253-3642. Web site: www-polisci.mit.edu/boston review.

Field, Rice Hall, Oberlin College, Oberlin, OH 44074, (216) 775-8408. This biannual publishes poetry, translations and essays by poets. According to *Poet's Market*, the publishers say they look for the best. It is a handsome, flat-spined edition.

The Georgia Review, The University of Georgia, Athens, GA 30602-9009, (706) 542-3481. According to *Poet's Market*, this journal has been nominated for awards along with slick national magazines like *The Atlantic* and *The New Yorker*. The poems and reviews are fine. They publish distinguished poets.

The Kenyon Review, Kenyon College, Gambier, OH 43022, (614) 427-5208. The Kenyon Review is a print review also on-line at ken yonreview@kenyon.edu.

Literal Latte is an on-line review at www.literal-latte.com

The Paris Review, 541 E. 72nd St., New York, NY 10021-4075, (718) 539-7085. *Poet's Market* calls this a distinguished quarterly that has published many of the major poets writing in English.

Ploughshares, Emerson College, Dept. M, 100 Beacon St., Boston, MA 02116. Ploughshares is a print review also at www.emerson.edu/ ploughshares/.

Poetry, 60 W. Walton St., Chicago, IL 60610, (312) 255-3703. *Poet's Market* cites this as probably the most prestigious magazine in which a poet can publish. Since its founding in 1912, it has been an international showcase publishing the biggest names.

Salon: An Interactive Magazine of the Arts, Books and Ideas. Web site: http://www.salon1999.com. Salon is a free on-line publication with major corporate sponsors. It has fine writing by well-known contemporary writers and poets.

These literary magazines are just a sample of the many fine ones available. There are many ways to increase your knowledge of literary magazines on your own. When you read a work by a particular poet or an anthology of poems, be sure to read the acknowledgment page, which tells where the poems were first published. Sometimes anthologies note the places of first publication in the contributor's notes. You may find out about magazines you've never heard of. The annual *The Best American Poetry* anthology, edited by David Lehman, always lists the magazines from which the poems were selected. This is true, too, for the annual Pushcart Prize anthologies edited by Bill Henderson in which winning poems and prose are published from approximately forty-four small press publications. Directories for submitting poems for publication, such as those included later in this chapter, are a good source for reading about literary magazines. In addition, a library reference journal called *Magazines for Libraries* has a special section on small press and literary magazines that describes each well.

Book Review Publications

The journals listed above publish reviews of poetry books, and reading lively poetry book reviews is important to broadening your knowledge of poetry. By reading as many as you can, you get to consider how experienced readers and writers of poetry look into particular poems and whole collections. You sharpen your own perceptions and appreciation of poetry and the craft of writing it. You become informed about the work of poets who may be new to you. Here is a listing of some worthwhile publications that publish poetry book reviews:

The Bloomsbury Review, 1762 Emerson St., Denver, CO 80218-1012; phone (303) 863-0406, fax (303) 863-0408. This review is published six times a year and an annual subscription costs $16. Well-written reviews of a fine selection of literature include many about poetry.

The Boston Book Review, 30 Brattle St., 4th Floor, Cambridge, MA 02138; phone (617) 497-0344, fax (617) 497-0394. An annual subscription costs $24, or $40 outside of the U.S., and includes ten issues. This review is also on-line free at http://www.bookwire.com/bbr-home.html and www.bostonbookreview.com/BBR.

The New York Review of Books, 250 W. 57th St., Suite 1321, New York, NY 10107. This one is also accessible on-line at http://www.nybooks.com. E-mail address is nyrev@panix.com.

The New York Times Book Review, 229 W. 43rd St., New York, NY 10036-3913, (212) 556-1234. While it is published with the Sunday edition of the paper, you can subscribe to just the review for $39 a year. Poetry books are usually reviewed by recognized contemporary poets.

The Small Press Review, Dustbooks, P.O. Box 100, CA 95967, (800) 477-6110. This monthly publication includes reviews of small press magazines and books. It would be hard to learn about the work of many poets published by the smaller presses anywhere else.

Look for *Hungry Mind Review*, *San Francisco Review of Books* and *Women's Review of Books* as well. In your search for good reviews, don't overlook the newsletters of your local booksellers. Often fine local poets and expert readers of poetry write the reviews. You may also have a local literary newsletter associated with an arts organization or poetry center. Make a point of subscribing to it or picking up a free copy at libraries and bookstores.

Materials for Self-Study

The Lannan Foundation, 5401 McConnell Ave., Los Angeles, CA 90066-7027, (800) 869-7573. Their catalog of Lannan Literary Videos lists the programs they have made of distinguished poets reading from their work and being interviewed. The videotapes are also distributed for libraries and organizations by the San Francisco Poetry Center's Archives (see "Centers") and for individuals by Small Press Distribution (see "Specialty Distributors"). Contact the Lannan Foundation for a catalog that lists and pictures the poets and gives ordering information. The videos are a reasonable $19.95 plus shipping (plus sales tax in California).

Poets on Poetry Series from the University of Michigan Press (P.O. Box 1104, Ann Arbor, MI 48106, (313) 764-4392), collects, as the catalog copy says, "critical books by contemporary poets, gathering the articles, interviews, and book reviews by which they have articulated the poetics of a new generation." With over fifty-eight volumes published or forthcoming, there are far too many to name here, but the whole series is fantastic. Go to or call your favorite poetry bookstore, visit your library or write the University of Michigan Press for a catalog.

Thin Air Video, Contemporary Poetry Archives, 58 East 4th St., #3, New York, NY 10003, (212) 254-2803. Director/archivist Mitch Corber has created an expansive New York City resource generated over a nine-year period of producing a weekly show for cable TV. The archives include footage categorized as the beat generation, New York school, women's vices, historic events and new trends. Tapes can be ordered by phone and cost $25 each; five or more are $20. Shipping is extra.

Voices and Visions, a series of self-study videotapes on famous American poets produced by the Annenberg Foundation, is available at libraries and through National Public Television. Walt Whitman, Emily Dickinson, Robert Frost, Wallace Stevens, William Carlos Williams, Ezra Pound, Marianne Moore, T.S. Eliot, Hart Crane, Langston Hughes, Elizabeth Bishop, Robert Lowell and Sylvia Plath are featured. In 1987, Random House published a companion book to the series called *The Poet in America*, edited by Helen Vendler. It includes information about the poets' lives and careers, and features a bibliography.

Watershed Foundation, 6925 Willow St. NW, No. 201, Washington, DC 20012, (202) 722-9105 or (800) 366-9105. This foundation produces and distributes audiotapes of poetry readings. The Signature Series is composed of retrospective readings by major poets reading their own work. The Touchstone Series is composed of tapes of younger, more performance-oriented poets. The Archive Series is composed of readings of the work of recently deceased major poets. Watershed offers a catalog of the audio cassettes.

Resource Magazines for Poets
Media Weavers, 1738 NE 24th, Portland, OR 97211. Subscription is $10 a year or $12 in Canada. A delightful quarterly publication dedicated to building the community of the printed word. Articles, profiles, ads and submission announcements are of great interest.

Poetry Flash: A Poetry Review and Literary Calendar for the West, P.O. Box 4172, Berkeley, CA 94704; phone (510) 525-5476, fax (510) 525-6752. Subscriptions are $16 a year for nine issues, $30 outside the U.S. This one is chock-full and hard to beat. It lists literary events all over the country, and has interviews, reviews and lots of ads from small presses.

Poets & Writers Magazine, 72 Spring St., New York, NY 10012, (212) 226-3586; Web site: http://www.pw.org. If you begin subscribing to (or finding in your library) this quarterly publication from the non-profit organization Poets and Writers, Inc., you will become aware of the various residency and low-residency poetry writing degree programs available in this country as well as the many continuing education-style writer's workshops and tutorials. You will also find articles of interest ranging from interviews with notable writers to information about organizations and foundations that support writers. You will read about poets who have won awards and you can add their books to your reading list. In addition, many fine presses, including our nation's university presses, advertise their new releases so you will become aware of books by today's recognized poets. (If these presses interest you, get your name on their mailing lists for catalogs and newsletters.) And *Poets & Writers Magazine* does a fine job of listing places seeking submissions and contest and award deadlines. In addition to the magazine, Poets & Writers, Inc. publishes a biennial *Directory of American Poets and Fiction Writers*, and a booklet listing literary bookstores among other publications.

Wordscape, 1634 11th Avenue, Seattle, WA 98122. A subscription is $15.00 a year for twelve monthly issues. *Wordscape* is devoted to promoting the literary arts in Washington State. It offers literary news, interviews with writers, reviews of books from north-west publishers, announcements of workshops, competitions and calls for submissions as well as a comprehensive calendar of literary events. There is useful information for poets everywhere, and this magazine stands as an excellent model for efforts in areas without such a resource.

Writer's Digest Magazine, 1507 Dana Avenue, Cincinnati, Ohio 45207, (800)888-6880. This magazine, available at most newsstands, has a monthly column on writing poetry by Michael Bugeja along with other feature articles and tip columns about writing and poetry. Each issue includes a list of publications and contests looking for submissions.

Poetry Centers

These resources exist in most regions of the country. They do not necessarily publish poetry, but collect contemporary poetry and make it available to the public through noncirculating libraries, lectures and readings, newsletters, videotapes and audio tapes. These centers and their archives and libraries are invaluable to serious writers of poetry. Their newsletters are filled with information about poetry and poets, and their Web sites are informative and linked to other poetry Web sites. Below I describe some of the bigger ones. Even if you don't live nearby, membership may be beneficial.

Also, contact your local arts commission or council and ask what resources are available to poets in your community. You can call one of these centers and ask if they have information about your area. Or you can check with creative writing offices at your local universities, colleges and continuing and extended education programs to see if they sponsor regular reading series, library collections, classes, lectures, contests, publications and awards.

The Loft, Pratt Community Center, 66 Malcolm Ave. SE, Minneapolis, MN 55414, (612) 379-8999; Web site: http://www.lof t.org. The Loft sponsors events, classes, workshops, a small press library, grants for writers and a newsletter called *A View From the Loft*, produced eleven times per year. On their Web site you will find a listing of all their programs and grants, registration forms for membership and excerpts from their newsletter. Membership is $40 a year, $20 for students and low-income people, $50 for households and $25 for those living outside the seven-county metropolitan area. The newsletter comes with the membership. The Small Press Library, which is always open when classes are in session, houses over 1,500 small press collections, anthologies and books about poetry as well as subscriptions to ninety literary journals. It has back issues of many journals of archival interest from which readers can see the development of literature in this country. There is an anthology of Loft student writing, a mentor reading series to provide area poets and fiction writers with advanced professional development opportunities, career development grants, summer opportunities for young writers, and a focus on activities for culturally diverse writers.

Poet House, 72 Spring St. (between Broadway and Lafayette), New York, NY 10012, (212) 431-7920. The Poet House has a 35,000-volume library open to the public from Tuesday through Friday, 11A.M. to 7P.M. and Saturday 11A.M. to 4P.M.. The library includes poetry books, reference materials, subscriptions to over one hundred literary journals, and a video- and audiotape collection. There are comfy couches, and people are meant to come and write. The center offers a once-a-year exhibition of new poetry publications, enters them into a directory and then adds them to the library's collection. A copy of the *Directory of American Poetry Books* is included with a membership of $40 a year. Membership also includes discounts to readings, lectures and the series called "Passwords" in which distinguished poets read and discuss the work of other poets.

The Poetry Center, San Francisco State University, 1600 Holloway, San Francisco, CA 94132, (415) 338-3132; Web site: http://www.SFS U.edu/~newlit/welcome.htm. Membership dues are $20 a year and entitle members to rent from the Center's extensive archive of poets on video- and audiotapes. Videotapes can be purchased for $45 and audiotapes for $15. The Center's tape catalog is on-line along with information about their internships, schedule of readings and archives. The Web site has audio clips, photos and links to other literary and poetry sites. Members receive the yearly magazine *Archive News*. The Center's reading room has over one thousand noncirculating volumes of poetry and books about poetry. The Center is one of two distributors for the Lannan Foundation's $19.95 videos about well-known poets. Organizations and libraries can call (415) 338-1056 for information on the tapes.

The Richard Hugo House, 1634 11th Avenue, Seattle, WA 98122; phone (206) 322-7030, fax (206) 320-8767; E-mail: admin@hugohous e.org. This new literary center has a commitment to "encouraging the development of writing as a craft and as a method of inquiry." The main floor is open to the public during scheduled hours. There are rotating gallery exhibits, a collection of underground magazines ("zines") from around the country and comfortable seating. An "upstairs pass" is $50 annually, $20 for students and seniors. This pass includes a newsletter, reduced fees and access to resources such as a library of current literary magazines, books by regional authors, reference books and a collection of submission guidelines. The center makes available reasonably priced on-site photocopying, faxing, E-mail and Internet access as well as quiet space for writers and literary groups, and an auditorium for readings by and conversations with new and well-known authors. The center is responsive to community needs. Volunteers have started an after-school reading program for at-risk children as well as programs for prisoners and homeless writers. Anyone with an idea for a literary event can submit a proposal and apply for facilities, staffing or other support. Space is offered for response group meetings, classes in various genres and master classes by well-known writers. Other activities include providing opportunities for parents to bring kids to seminars on poetry and music, and sponsoring grants for writers to help them research books. The center also pays writers for teaching classes to seniors.

The University of Arizona Poetry Center, 1216 N. Cherry Ave., P.O. Box 210410, Tucson, AZ 85719-0410; phone (520) 321-7760, fax (520) 621-5566, Web site: http://www.coh.arizona.edu/poetry/. If you are lucky enough to live near Tucson, this center is one of the richest resources you will find. It is a library full of volumes of poetry, issues of literary magazines and videotapes of distinguished poets reading from their work. You are welcome to spend hours in the library reading and viewing its resources. With grants from local foundations and the Academy of American Poets, the center also hosts a writing residency, poetry reading series and student poetry contest, and prints a fine newsletter with articles and interviews of interest to poets, particularly poets in the southwest.

The Writer's Center, 4508 Walsh St., Bethesda, MD 20815; phone (301) 654-8664, fax (301) 654-8667; Web site: http://www.writer.org. This center offers workshops, readings, a bimonthly newsletter called *Carrousel*, a quarterly literary magazine called *Poet Lore*, and a bookstore featuring poetry and literary magazines and books on writing. The Web site features a writer's registry and job board, a literary events calendar, workshop brochure, parts of the organization's newsletter *Carrousel* and hot links to other poetry and literary sites.

National Government Resources and Offices

National Center for the Book, The Library of Congress, 101 Independence Ave. SE, #650, Washington, DC 20540-8200; phone (202) 707-5221, fax (202) 707-0269. The center promotes appreciation of books, libraries and reading by working in conjunction with state centers. Check with a library in one of your state's larger cities to find out if you have a state center for the book, or call the National Center for the Book for information. State centers sponsor readings, salons and reading groups.

Poetry and Literature Center, The Library of Congress, 10 First St. SE, Washington, DC 20540-8910; phone (202) 707-5394, fax (202) 707-9946. This is the office that appoints the poet laureate of the

United States. It is good to check each year to see what special projects the poet laureate is fostering and what materials and events are associated with it. This office arranges for poets to record readings of their work for the library's tape archives. The office also advises libraries on literary programs and materials.

Poetry-Only Bookstores

Groliers Poetry Bookshop, Louisa Solano, proprietor, 6 Plympton Street, Cambridge, MA 02138; phone (617) 547-4648 or (800) 234-POEM, fax (617) 547-4230. Established in 1927, this is the oldest all-poetry bookshop in the nation. T.S. Eliot frequented the shop as did many other famous poets. Ms. Solano has over fifteen thousand volumes of poetry and one hundred books about poetry on the store's shelves. If the list of what you are looking for is long, fax Groliers the list, or call to discuss what you are looking for. The store sponsors a reading series that takes place at Harvard. Calendars of the readings can be sent to Massachusetts state residents. The store advertises a yearly poetry contest in *Poets & Writers Magazine* for poets who have not yet published a book of poems.

Open Books, A Poem Emporium, 2414 N. 45th St., Seattle, WA 98103; phone (206) 633-0811, fax (206) 633-3978. Devoted to new/used/out-of-print poetry and related titles, the store is open Tuesday through Saturday, 11A.M. to 6P.M., (Pacific Standard Time); on Fridays, it's open until 8P.M.. Owners Christine Deavel and John W. Marshall both hold MFA's in poetry from the University of Iowa. They have extensive knowledge of poets, poetry and small press publications. They can help you find new as well as used and out-of-print editions of most published poetry. They handle books of prose on poetry, directories of poetry publications and literary poetry journals.

If you try to call them, you may get their voice mail. Instead, they recommend faxing them with your request or sending a postcard. They can help you clarify the names of titles and poets, and they keep a wish list for customers who are looking for specific books. Although they don't do book searches, they stay alert for the titles particular customers desire and notify them if that title comes in. They often buy remainders and notify customers from their mailing list that books are available at a low price as well as mention new titles they have acquired. If you get in touch with them, they will respond by fax or postcard.

Their newsletter lists recently acquired titles and forthcoming titles, as well as sample poems and a listing of sponsored readings. The proprietors will mail books USPS and charge only the actual freight. They special order any title, and if you buy twelve books or tapes, you receive the average price of them in credit. There is a 10 percent discount if five or more copies of the same title are ordered at one time. They have gift certificates and complimentary gift wrap.

Specialty Distributor

Small Press Distribution, 1341 7th St., Berkeley, CA 94710; phone (800) 869-7553 or (510) 524-1668; E-mail: spd@igc.apc.org. This distributor has detailed catalogs available. The listings include books of contemporary poetry and fiction, cultural studies, multicultural authors and gay and lesbian writings. Individuals can call to order Lannan Foundation poetry videotapes.

Conferences, Workshops and Retreats

William Noble has put together a book called *The Complete Guide to Writer's Conferences and Workshops*, (Chicago; Eriksson; 1995). He lists events in more than forty states as well as Canada. Writer's conferences and workshops offer poets the opportunity to study under the guidance of well-known poets over periods of time usually ranging from one day to ten days. Get on the mailing list for conferences in your area or in areas you'd like to travel to because the workshop descriptions keep you aware of poets and their publications as well as entice you to use your vacation time to study and concentrate on your writing.

Poets & Writers, Inc. publishes an annual list of two hundred workshops complete with information on workshop leaders, dates, addresses, fees and deadlines. It is called *Writer's Conferences: An Annual Guide to Literary Conferences* and is available directly through Poets & Writers, Inc. Their address is on page 165.

In addition to the exchange of ideas on poetry writing, seclusion and time are necessary to invent, shape and edit your work. It used to be more difficult to find out where writer's colonies and retreats were located and who sponsored them. Now much of this information has been collected in a reference book entitled *Artists & Writers Colonies: Retreats, Residencies, and Respites for the Creative Mind* by Gail Hellund Bowler. It was published in 1995 by Blue Heron Publishing, Inc., 24450 NW Hansen Rd., Hillsboro, OR 97124, (503) 621-3911. The entries contain all of the information you will need to decide if you should apply or write for more information. As the author suggests, first look for places closest to home as many of the colonies only offer space, time and money to local or regional residents. After looking at local or regional colonies, then look geographically further afield.

Professional Organizations

The Academy of American Poets, 584 Broadway, Suite 1208, New York, NY 10012-3250; phone (212) 274-0343, fax (212) 274-9427; Web site: http://www.poets.org; E-mail: poets@artswire.org. There are varying levels of annual membership. The $25 contributing membership includes a year's subscription to *American Poet*. The $45 associate membership includes complimentary admission to readings in New York and other cities, as well as hardcover editions of the books chosen for the Walt Whitman Award and the James Laughlin Award, which are mailed annually. Higher levels of membership include tapes of readings, other award-winning books and publications, and invitations to readings and receptions.

Associated Writing Programs, Tallwood House, Mail Stop 1E3, George Mason University, Fairfax, VA 22030; phone (703) 993-4301, fax (703) 993-4302; Web site: http://www.gmu.edu/departments/ awp. The Web site tells about member schools and writing programs with links to each school's Web site. The organization publishes a directory through Dustbooks (P.O. Box 100, Paradise, CA 95967, [800] 477-6110) called *Official AWP Guide to Writing Programs*. It features extensive information on writing programs, colonies, conferences and centers throughout the U.S., Canada, and Europe, and is indexed by region and subject. You can find out what is happening at colleges and universities in your area.

The organization holds a national annual three-day conference, and most importantly, the organization publishes a fine newsletter called *The AWP Chronicle* six times a year. It is available with a $55 a year membership or separately for $20 for six issues, $32 for twelve issues, slightly higher in Canada. *The AWP Chronicle* is an open forum for the debate and examination of current issues in contemporary letters, and the teaching of creative writing. It has a good list of awards, contests, publication submission and grant deadlines as well as conferences, colonies and workshops all over the U.S. Its "Books by Members" listing in each issue is informative.

The International Women's Writing Guild, P.O. Box 810, Gracie Station, New York, NY 10028; phone (212) 737-7536, fax (212) 737-9469; Web site: http://www.iwwg.com; E-mail: iwwg@wwg .com. This organization, which is open to men, has a mission to be a constantly expanding network for the personal and professional empowerment of women through writing. Membership of $35 annually includes a frequently updated list of literary agents, independent small presses and services for writers; a subscription to *Network*, a thirty-two-page newsletter published six times a year; access to health insurance plans available to individual members at group rates; participation in nationwide conferences, regional writing workshops, cluster groups and round-robin manuscript exchanges.

National Association for Poetry Therapy, P.O. Box 551, Port Washington, NY 11050, (516) 944-9791. Membership includes the quarterly *Journal of Poetry Therapy*, and the *NAPT Museletter* published three times a year. Dues are $60 annually. The association is composed of poets and therapists who believe that writing poetry is healing. Their conferences, workshops and publications emphasize practical approaches to helping people write poetry.

The Poetry Society of America, 15 Gramercy Park, New York, NY 10003, (212) 254-9628. The PSA, which is the oldest poetry organization in the U.S., offers eleven annual awards, seminars, workshops, readings, festivals and programs that get poetry into the public eye on subways, TV and the Internet. Events of regional interest are organized and hosted by PSA affiliates in California, Florida, New York, Illinois, Mississippi and Washington, DC. It is responsible for getting the Pulitzer Prize in Poetry established in 1922. Membership dues begin at $25 for students. Benefits include reduced admission to PSA events, free application to PSA poetry contests and the twice-yearly PSA newsletter and calendar.

More Useful Web Sites

Most literary Web sites have links to other Web sites of interest to poets and writers. I have already mentioned the first one listed below, so you may have already found your way to these Web sites.

The Academy of American Poets, http://www.poets.org, has audio clips of poets from Yeats, Auden and Frost among more contemporary voices.

Ann Arbor Poetry Forum is at www.poetryforum.org. It broadcasts poetry and interviews. You can get more information at E-mail: allears@poetryforum.org or by writing P.O. Box 7141, Ann Arbor, MI 48107.

Literary Leap features a carefully selected group of links to useful on-line resources for writers. It is a service of the Western States Art Federation and is available at http:/www.westaf.org.

Northwest Bookfest, www.speakeasy.org/nwbookfest. This Web site offers monthly book reviews and names of regional literary presenters and associations.

Poetry Leap is at Web site www.poems.com and features poems, poets, books and interviews, articles on poetry and an archive of poems from previous issues.

Speakeasy: New Writing From Seattle & Elsewhere, http://www.speakeasy.org/subtext/. This electronic publication offers poems and information on the literary scene and workshops.

Switched-On Gutenberg, An Electronic Journal of the English-Speaking World, http://weber.u.washington.edu/~jnh/. This is edited by poet Jana Harris at Academic Programs, University of Washington Extension.

FORMING AND USING A WRITER'S GROUP

Sharing early efforts and works in progress with other writers is a satisfying and useful way to spend some of your writing time. Groups meet anywhere from once a week to once a month. They usually have six to fifteen people in them. They meet in people's homes, and in rooms in libraries and cafés. Sometimes the groups function as writing circles where writing exercises are done at the group meeting, and sometimes they are response groups only. Some groups may be composed of poets only and some may have people writing in any genre.

The best way to create a writing group is to attend a writing workshop in your area and see if people in the class would like to continue to meet. I know people who have enjoyed membership in the national organization, the International Women's Writing Guild, which maintains a list of members by zip code and promotes local writing groups and circles. Local bookstores, coffeehouses, arts commissions, literary newsletters, church groups, in-house groups at your workplace, neighborhood libraries and State Centers for the Book may have knowledge of local writing groups seeking members.

Once you create or join a group, make a list of the members' names, phone numbers and addresses so that ride and cancellation arrangements can be made.

Here are the elements of a good writing group:

1. As many members as possible bring a piece of writing to the group for response each time.

2. Each member offers a response to each piece of writing presented.

3. Each member reads to the group (members may read along from copies if the writer desires) and then listens to the group's response without commenting or interrupting.

4. After the response is finished, the writer can ask for further clarification.

5. Response time should be fairly divided among the presenting members, so someone needs to be a good timekeeper.

The three key elements here are: "response" (not criticism), "each," and "listens to the group's response without commenting or interrupting."

It is most helpful to hear how your writing affects your readers/ listeners by learning:

1. what words and phrases stick

2. what feelings are elicited when the readers/listeners hear the writing

3. which of those feelings draw them out of the writing and why

4. any way that they are not satisfied and are curious to know more

Natalie Goldberg always started her response time in workshops by having listeners merely "say back" to the writer words and phrases they heard, without any discussion. This allowed the writer to truly experience how their writing made contact. Next, the group could talk about how they felt as a result of hearing the whole piece, and then how they felt in parts of it. We have many ways of describing feelings, and groups may have to practice articulating them by saying, for example, "I felt such and such when I read these words" rather than, "I have a problem with . . ." or "This doesn't work for me," or "You must change this." It is much more informative for the writer to hear, "I was brought too quickly from this sad feeling to this joke, and I felt cheated that I couldn't honor the sad feeling," or "I was totally immersed in the scene, and then suddenly I felt removed from or kept out of being there."

Some people continue to call their writing groups critique groups and say they offer constructive criticism. I don't like the word "critique" in relation to helping writers with works in progress. The etymology of the word "criticize" means to tear apart. Writing is too much of an organic experience for cutting apart to be helpful in fostering its generation. The writer might trim something, leave behind a shell or have a new piece rise out of the ashes of a first attempt, but it is the writer who gets to decide this. Good decisions are made on the basis of hearty, honest response rather than on someone else's idea of how to fix something.

Another benefit of this response method is that no one can start to take over by telling the writer how to fix something, or by showing off copyediting skills when the writer is still in the invention or shaping stage.

When each member shares his or her response, even if only to second what someone else has said or to make it known that his or her response differs from others, the group is strong because each member is equally valuable to the group. It takes courage to be in a writing group—courage to share your work, to trust your responses to someone else's work, and to verbalize them. All of these elements must be present if the group is to work well.

When you listen to responses to your work, do not interrupt. Once you interrupt, the group of readers/listeners is no longer responding to the writing but to you. We do not go into the world with our publications to explain them, add more to them or correct our readers' misperceptions. The writing itself must do the work. Be sure you give responders your ear and let them respond to the *writing*. Usually a piece of writing is discussed for ten to twenty minutes, and then you can ask the group for clarification. If you meant one feeling but another emerged, you may want to investigate how that happened. At any rate, go home with notes from everyone's responses to your writing and then sit down and decide how to develop your work.

It is hard to respond to something as sensitive as someone's new poetry. So always thank your listeners for sharing what they thought and felt and wondered. And never argue with them. You can decide which information to use, but always make your listeners realize you want to hear what they as the first audience have to say. That way you will always get valuable information.

A final note: Although writer's groups may spend some time each meeting sharing news about members' work accepted for publication and announcements about deadlines, contests, events and organizations, members must be careful not to let discussion take away from response time. Writer's groups are primarily to help writers keep writing. Also, they must avoid buoying up floundering egos, spending too much time excusing away rejections and sympathizing with complaints about not enough time to write. Some people (and each of us becomes this person at some time or another) are so frightened of writing and listening to response that they distract the group's attention with writing-related issues and stall the work on writing itself.

I know of writing groups that have offered joint public readings of their work and created joint publications. They have hired professionals from time to time to facilitate their group or gone en masse to a writer's workshop or conference. They have shared subscriptions to useful journals. There really are a variety of ways that writing groups can foster their members' writing.

PUBLISHING YOUR POEMS

When you feel you are ready to have an editor see your work, begin making submissions to small press literary magazines or local poetry contests. You can read about them in directories and newsletters. Here are some that are readily available in bookstores and libraries:

Directory of Literary Magazines. Complete Information on More Than 600 U.S. and Foreign Magazines That Publish Poetry, Fiction, and Essays.

This reasonably priced directory lists only quality literary magazines. It is published by the Council of Literary Magazines and Small Presses through Moyer Bell Limited, Wakefield, Rhode Island.

International Directory of Little Magazines & Small Presses, Dustbooks, P.O. Box 100 Paradise, CA 95967, (800) 477-6110. This directory lists over 6000 publications in the U.S., Wales, Britain, and Canada. Publications are indexed by subject, theme, type of poetry, and region, making this a good resource for writers who want to locate appropriate magazines for their submissions. Entries represent national consumer and small literary markets.

Poet's Market, Writer's Digest Books, 1507 Dana Ave., Cincinnati, OH 45207, (513) 531-2222. Published annually, this reference book lists over 1,800 publications representing national consumer and small literary markets, and includes practical information and interviews with industry professionals on making submissions and understanding the editorial process. Additionally, this directory lists grants, contests and awards, retreats and workshops. Magazines and presses are indexed by subject and geographical location as well as alphabetically.

In addition to these directories, there are the publications I wrote about earlier that list current calls for submissions to magazines and contests: *Poets & Writers Magazine, Writer's Digest Magazine, The AWP Chronicle, Poetry Flash* and *Wordscape.* Your local arts scene or arts commission newsletters might also have listings, and newsletters from poetry centers may list submissions wanted. Checking the bulletin boards at your local college's creative writing offices can also help you locate places to which you can submit your work.

Locating places to submit your poems is, however, only half the work. If possible, you should read a back issue or two of the magazine you intend to send your poems to and see if your poems fit there. It is usually wise to first submit your work to local publications and build a publication history before you try prestigious or nationally distributed magazines.

Your submission should have three to six poems in it. It must be typed with one per page. An editor can get a better sense of your voice from reading at least three poems, but always arrange the poems by putting the ones first that you feel are the best. Make sure your name and address are at the top of each page unless a publication or contest particularly requests you not do that. Mail the submission with a short cover letter and self-addressed stamped envelope (SASE). If there is no need to return the copies (sometimes photocopying is cheaper than adequate return postage), say so in your cover letter and put only a first-class stamp on the SASE so you can receive notification of acceptance or rejection.

Your cover letter should mention the titles of the poems enclosed and, in no more than three sentences, share something about yourself, such as where you work or what your special interests are. Do not say who your teachers were or list more than four or five previous publication credits. Editors will not respond to requests to comment on your work. They sometimes write a comment if they decide they want to. Editors of literary publications are often poets themselves taking time out of their writing schedule to keep a literary magazine going. They have other jobs as well and are swamped with hundreds of submissions.

How many places should you submit your poems to? Unless publications state they accept simultaneous submissions, it is still the practice to send particular poems to one editor at a time. This can be slow going, and editors may request up to three months to respond to your work. If you haven't heard from an editor after three months, call or write to see how they are coming and to ask for a decision. Be sure to name the titles of the poems you submitted. If you do submit your work to several editors at once, you are obligated to notify the other editors if a piece is accepted by one of the publications. However, when you notify any editors who have not said simultaneous submissions are all right, you may disgruntle them. To keep your records straight, keep a log of submissions and dates, or a folder of copies of your cover letters.

Many editors tell you in a hand-scrawled note on a rejection slip that they would like another chance to see your work. Believe them and send some other poems immediately or in the future. If they publish you, be sure to submit more poems. These editors are usually interested in ongoing relationships with poets whose work they admire.

The best way to keep your work circulating is to follow these guidelines and keep good records of what is out to whom. Then follow through if you haven't heard from an editor, and make honest assessments about resubmitting the same work to another magazine or continuing to work on the poems that have not been accepted. Sometimes just having been parted from the poem for awhile or knowing that it has been read by a stranger allows you to see things that need revising that you hadn't seen before.

BUILDING AND PUBLISHING A COLLECTION

Poets usually think in terms of publishing individual poems. Usually only after eighteen to thirty to forty of them have appeared individually in publications might the poet submit these poems to a press for publication as a chapbook. Chapbook is the name for a short collection, inexpensively produced with a paper cover and frequently bound with stitching or staples. The term "chapbook" comes from the hawking of early booksellers in England after the printing press was invented. They would sell paper books from pockets cut into the insides of their wool overcoats. They would walk the streets calling, "Cheap books, cheap books."

After the publication of a chapbook, the poet continues to publish new poems individually. These may become another chapbook, or collections of forty-eight to sixty to eighty poems might be submitted as a booklength manuscript for publication. After several books have appeared in a poet's career, a publisher will sometimes put out an edition of his or her new poems and selected poems from past editions. A press might publish poems posthumously as well as do an edition of the complete collected poems by the author. Often it is people close to the poet such as colleagues, lifelong editors, or family who help put this together.

How does a poet start making chapbook or first book submissions to publishers? First of all, poets must trust that although each poem might appear to be separate from other poems in subject, appearance on the page and images, themes appear when a substantial number of poems by the same author are published together in a book. It becomes clear what concerns and questions a poet is obsessed with and exploring. An order presents itself in which to arrange the poems in a book, even if it is not the order in which the poems were written. Though the poet usually makes the first pass at ordering the poems for a collection, ultimately the editor has a large hand in figuring out the final order and which poems will be included.

In an article in the July 1997 literary newsletter *Wordscape*, Seattle editor Robert Ward, who publishes the bimonthly literary publication *Bellowing Ark*, was quoted as saying he reads between 150 and

300 submissions for every issue of his magazine and sometimes offers his critical comments and accolades to the writers. In addition to his magazine, he has published twenty-five volumes of poetry and fiction "by invitation only." When he invites a writer to do so, he will work closely with interested writers to develop their work into book form.

This is a common way that poets build a collection. My first book was published by Duckabush Press, the companion press to the literary magazine, *The Duckabush Review*. In this case, I noticed that the editor took several of my poems every time I made a submission. When I thought I had published enough poems in his magazine as well as in other literary magazines, I wrote him a letter explaining that I felt I had a booklength manuscript and wondered whether he might be interested in publishing it. He agreed to publish it, and worked with me to make the book a strong one, selecting from my new poems as well as including some that had previously appeared in a chapbook. I advise you to start publishing locally and establish a relationship with an editor by regularly submitting poems if the editor shows an interest in your work. Find out what articles the editor may have written on poetry, read them and send a note to the editor about your appreciation for his ideas and the editorial job he does on his publication. Finally, when you are ready, write a letter asking the editor if he or she would be interested in seeing your manuscript. Be sure to include a list of the publications in which any of the poems first appeared.

When preparing a chapbook or booklength manuscript for submission, include a front page with the collection's title and your name, address and phone number; an acknowledgment page; and a table of contents. Mail the manuscript in a manila envelope and enclose a cover letter and SASE.

Literary newsletters and resource magazines routinely list poetry chapbook and booklength manuscript contests. Although there is usually a reading fee attached to entering your manuscript, doing a certain number of these a year if you feel you have a manuscript ready is the best way to circulate your work among people likely to publish poetry.

Another way to see about getting published is to attend writers' conferences and workshops, and sign up for any offerings on small press publishing. Here you will meet the editors and publishers, see what they publish, learn about presses and learn how to figure out which ones might be interested in your work.

Finally, there are grants that help writers develop their work and assist in the costs of the actual publication. The National Endowment for the Humanities (202/606-8400) offers grants that could be of interest to serious poets as does the National Endowment for the Arts (202/682-5400). Both of these organizations help fund local and regional grants, and many local and regional organizations and presses also offer grants or have contests. These can be located by looking at the contests and awards sections of the resource magazines and directories mentioned earlier, and in the directories described later in this chapter.

In this country where market sales drive publishing (since fewer people read poetry and buy poetry books, fewer publishers allocate funds to acquire and publish poetry), there are a growing number of flourishing poetry presses. Keep informed about contests, grants, editors and presses, but most importantly, don't let anything (including rejection) get in the way of writing your poems, shaping them and sending them out one by one. Although no one can honestly say your chances of being selected for publication are high, one thing leads to another. But the most important thing is to create poems, find editors who like them and, if you are lucky, win an award or prize here and there. All of this will increase the likelihood that a publisher will publish your book.

And, there is always self-publishing. If you believe there is an audience for your poems, investigate the costs of self-publishing, from using the quick-production facilities at Kinko's and Sudden Printing to finding a printer, binder, book designer and cover artist among your friends, relatives and connections. There are books on self-publishing, directory listings of self-publishers that might be resources for you, and speakers on self-publishing at writers conferences. *Books-in-Print* lists ninety-five titles on self-publishing as of 1997. Check with the Writer's Digest Book Club (1507 Dana Ave., Cincinnati, OH 45207; 513/531-8250) for titles, or ask your librarian for recommendations on resources for self-publishing.

Many editors suggest avoiding vanity presses because they charge the self-publishing poet quite a bit. Although they promise to do the marketing, they are in unfocused and ineffective in that effort. However, some self-publishing or copublishing organizatons are reputable and effective. Reading books on self-publishing helps you analyze the value of a vanity press, and informs you of what you are getting into with production, sales, marketing and distribution and what it should cost to do your book.

Any current issue of *Poetry Flash* from Berkeley, California, will most likely have ads for chapbook self-publishing services such as Concord, CA's A & E Press and Small Poetry Press, and The Poetry Center Press in Orinda, California.

Perhaps there is an organization in your community that would be interested in creating a book of your poems for their members. Perhaps you can join with other poets to form a cooperative venture to publish books of your group's work. This has been done successfully in many areas of the country and some of these co-ops have become distinguished presses! When the desire strikes, there are many options.

Here are some directories and books that might help you find an interested editor/publisher. Unless you are submitting a manuscript to an announced contest, first send a query letter to find out if the editor is interested in seeing unsolicited manuscripts. Briefly describe yours in your query and just as briefly describe yourself, listing any poetry awards or publications to your credit. Always include a SASE for the editor's reply. Do not expect an answer if you do not enclose this. Even so, busy, overworked editors may not get around to answering you. You can call or inquire by mail after three months have passed. This process is often thankless, so do it when you are psyched and consider any answers as progress. Figure that the postage, envelopes and time are just part of the expense of this business, just like the notebooks you use for writing. Book manuscripts are regularly multiply submitted, so if you find interest from more than one editor, don't hesitate to send the manuscripts to each of them for consideration!

The Directory of Editors lists editors and publishers with name, address and phone number. It also includes self-publishers.

The Directory of Poetry Publishers has twenty-one pieces of information on each of over two thousand book and magazine publishers of poetry including university presses. Editorial biases are described.

Dustbooks, P.O. Box 100, Paradise, CA 95967, (800) 477-6110. Dustbooks publishes three books that might be useful as you consider publishing a collection of your poems.

The Portable Writers Conference, edited by Stephen Blake Mettee, is a 450-page guide to getting and staying published that is written by forty-five editors, agents and authors.

In considering whether to query a press about your work, if a press says it publishes only residents of certain areas or work on certain subjects, be sure that you and your work qualify. Do not expect an answer if you query a press that is obviously not set up to use your work. I am cofounding editor of *The Poem and the World*, a yearly publication of poetry from Seattle and twenty-two cities around the world formally designated as her sister cities. We only publish poetry from these cities, yet we are regularly sent manuscripts and queries from people in all parts of the U.S. with no SASE included. An all-volunteer staff of students and writers, we do not have the time or budget to answer these letters and we don't. When an SASE is included, if someone has time, we may send a short note explaining we are not publishing poems by poets from any place in the U.S. other than the Seattle area.

GIVING READINGS AND PARTICIPATING IN LITERARY EVENTS

In my experience, poetry is read at bookstores, at arts and book festivals, on public and community radio and TV, at community college media centers, photography exhibits, museum events, galleries, coffeehouses, taverns, YMCA's and YWCA's, bed and breakfasts, schools, theaters, literacy programs, teen centers, parks, PTA meetings, Web sites and shopping centers. Poems have appeared on buses, subways, calendars, datebooks, posters, postcards and as public art in the stone and steps of public buildings. There is an organization in New York honoring the late poet Joseph Brodsky's idea of getting poetry into phone books.

If you want to become a reader at public series, find out who the series coordinators are and ask if they would be interested in seeing some of your poems with an eye toward inviting you to read. Better yet, if there is an open mike associated with a reading or event, participate. An open mike is an event in which an invited reader reads first, and audience members who have signed up to share their writing get a certain amount of time. Always adhere to the time limitations. No matter how much better you believe your poems are or how starved you are for an audience, it is unfair to use more than the allotted time. Doing so won't earn you any credits with the event coordinator or the audience, which will be saturated with listening.

If a series coordinator is interested in considering you as a featured reader, let them know in person or a cover letter what performance or reading experience you have had. When you do your reading, remember that you owe your poems and your audience a good job— read slowly and audibly. The kind of shyness or humility that leads to mumbling or reading too quickly or softly shortchanges the people who have decided to spend their time listening to you. So believe in them if not in yourself!

Before you begin, briefly tell your audience something about yourself and your delight to be included in the evening's event. If you can, it is a good gesture to tie your reading to some of the thoughts shared by previous readers. Be sure to pause between poems. Audiences have emotional reactions and need time to experience them before they can listen to the next poem. Sometimes it is a good idea to introduce particular poems by saying where you were when you wrote them or why you are reading them this evening. Attend readings and register your feelings about how other poets present their work. Learn from both their strengths and weaknesses.

If you want to participate as an organizer of poetry functions, you will certainly find a place for yourself. Start by attending poetry functions in your area. See how you like them. Would you like to join in that effort or does your experience make you want to explore creating your own function? Do you want to start a newsletter, local magazine, reading series or print series to get poetry into the public eye? Which particular people and organizations would you like to work with? What is your mission—the purpose of your program— and what are its requirements in terms of location, personnel, funding, publicity and dissemination? Who would most likely be interested enough to lend a hand with time, materials or money? Do you believe in this project enough to give it the time it will take away from your writing, and the thought and energy it will take to convince others to participate?

Why would anyone use what little time they may have for writing to take on a literary event project? For many reasons. If you write poetry, you probably rejoice in being surrounded by people who appreciate poetry. It feels good to participate rather than being alone writing and/or wallowing in the multitude of rejection letters all poets receive. It feels good to be getting instant gratification from grateful fellow coordinators and audiences instead of waiting for an acceptance. Creating a poetry event can put you in contact with fine poets, people committed to developing themselves as poets and people who are supportive of poetry. Creating a poetry event can force you to find out about the larger world of resources for deepening your abilities with the craft. And finally, creating poetry events can sometimes lead to professional work in a field that you love.

While I was an English instructor at a community college, I took the faculty advisory position to the school's literary magazine. After three years and three issues, I learned a lot about editorial work and publishing. When our county bus company created a poetry bus project and was looking for a curator, I applied and got the job partly based on my publication experience. When a former student of mine approached me about starting a poetry anthology, his fervor generated interest in me and together we launched *The Poem and the World*. For years it has received grants from various arts commissions and corporations. Being cofounding editor has taught me about marketing, book distribution and promotion. These skills have helped me with the sales of my own books, and being an editor has been a good credential on my resumé. Organizing the readings for each new publication has kept my name before people who look for individual readers for their programs.

April is National Poetry Month, and as a result, it has more poetry-related events than the other months of the year. These events are planned well in advance, so they are among the community projects that might interest you right away. Look at April editions of community newspapers, magazines and newsletters to see which organizations have sponsored poetry events. Events are coordinated nationwide by the Academy of American Poets along with other national and local sponsors such as educational associations, bookstores, presses, publications, media groups, libraries, YMCA's and foundations. Check with your local arts commission, arts council or library to see what is happening in your town. If nothing is happening and you want to begin a yearly celebration of poetry, get on-line at http://www.poets.org to see what events are proposed nationally and how you can get sponsorship for events in your community.

Many cities enjoy book festivals. In Seattle, Northwest Bookfest happens every year in October, and volunteers put together panels of writers to give presentations. Check if your community has a similar festival and find out how you can help create the programming. As I listed earlier in this chapter, Northwest Bookfest maintains a year-round Web site at www.speakeasy.org/nwbookfest with monthly book reviews, lists of regional literary presenters, associations and more. Perhaps you can get some ideas for your community and find some helpful links to other Internet sites.

◆ ◆ ◆

However you decide to go about things, may you find an exciting place for both your poems and your ideas!

CONTRIBUTOR'S NOTES

Meg Agnew lives in Seattle with her husband and two children. With a master's degree in education, she taught elementary school children for many years and now teaches hatha yoga to adults. Her interests include literature, tennis, hiking and skiing the mountains of the Northwest.

Denise Benitez is a yoga instructor in soggy Seattle. She says, "For me, language and writing are a way of placing myself in the world and of nourishing my soul."

Terry Chambers was born near San Francisco and schooled at the University of California Berkeley in the days of Mario Savio and magic bus. He built a sailboat and spent two years in timeless, un-reachable places. Now, after twenty years as a contractor building houses on the West Coast, he is resettling in the Southwest where he will "write and teach and celebrate wide open spaces."

Liz Gamberg, who taught mathematics for twelve years, is a potter and a new writer of poetry although she's been savoring others' poems for many years. She is currently testing software. She left the East Coast in 1980 in a fit of wanderlust and has been living in Seattle ever since.

Esther Altshul Helfgott writes and teaches writing in Seattle. She has a doctorate of philosophy in history, but made the decision not to use Ph.D. after her name except when writing about psychoanalysis because she thinks that as a writer/poet, it means nothing. Ever energetic, Esther founded and coordinates the iT'S aBOUT tIME wRITERS' rEADING sERIES in Seattle.

Diana Madaras is a Tucson, Arizona, entrepreneur who sold two of her three businesses to devote herself "almost full time" to her watercolor painting. Writing poems to complement her paintings became her primary focus in 1997, and she is working on a book that will combine both art forms. She is married, has five cats and holds a bachelor of science from Douglass College and a Master of Science from the University of Arizona.

Wanda Mawhinney, a twenty-five-year resident of Tucson, is a neuromuscular therapist and yoga teacher. She has been writing seriously for about two years. She hopes to write a book and keeps a daily journal for inspiration.

Marilyn Meyer is a writer, editor and teacher in Seattle. Her poems, essays, reviews and articles have been published in Northwest periodicals and literary magazines. She is the mother of three children and a wonder dog named Daisy. She enjoys gardening, camping, bicycling and reading.

Bev Parsons' passion is playing the piano. She also writes and enjoys theater and art. After working for many years in Seattle as a secretary for an insurance company, she has moved to the Caribbean.

Judy Tough and her husband Jim moved to Port Townsend, Washington, from Ohio in 1996 to camp, hike and enjoy nature. A retired child development professional and early childhood teacher, she is a daughter, mother, feminist, human services and environmental activist whose previously published writing was confined to letters to the editor.

Gary Winans has lived in West Seattle for fifteen years. He shares with his three children a joy of gardening, boardsailing in Puget Sound and chasing butterflies. He is active in a neighborhood project to restore Longfellow Creek and teaches elementary school children what "critters" are consumed by young salmon in streams and lakes. His poems appear in many literary magazines and public arts projects including *Bellowing Ark*, *Arnazella*, *Pudding House*, *The Poem and the World II*, and *Metro Bus Poetry 97 and 98*.

HOW-TO BOOKS ON WRITING POETRY

Behn, Robin and Chase Twichell. *The Practice of Poetry: Writing Exercises From Poets Who Teach*. New York: HarperCollins, 1992. Poetry writing ideas tested in the classroom by famous contemporary American poets including William Matthews, Stephen Dunn, Stanley Plumly, Molly Peacock, Rita Dove and Anne Waldman.

Bugeja, Michael J. *The Art and Craft of Poetry*. Cincinnati, OH: Writer's Digest Books, 1994. The book aims to help its audience compose and publish good poems and to ease them into the literary world. Dozens of poems included to illustrate the techniques addressed.

―――. *Creating Poetry*. Cincinnati, OH: Writers Digest Books, 1991. Beginning poems, using word combinations and new forms, applying lessons from other poets and poems, choosing and using images, using your poetic voice and finishing.

―――. *Poet's Guide: How to Publish and Perform Your Work*. Brownsville, OR: Story Line Press, 1995. The author and over twenty guest poets offer advice on workshops, readings, contests, magazines, revising, assembling and publishing. Includes exercises and literary and publishing terms.

Cohn, Myra. *Poem-Making: Ways to Begin Writing Poetry*. New York: HarperCollins, 1991. Meant for young readers, this is a handbook of the mechanics of writing poetry. It is clearly written and introduces new writers to rhyme, sound, metrics and some of the most common forms of poetry.

Deutsch, Babette. *A Poetry Handbook: A Dictionary of Terms*, 4th Edition. New York: Funk and Wagnalls, 1974. Long thought to be the definitive lexicon on terms concerning poetry, its forms and techniques.

Drury, John. *The Poetry Dictionary*. Cincinnati, OH: Story Press, 1995. Lots of useful information for practicing poets including elements of poetry, traditions and movements in poetry, forms and tools of the craft.

Ferra, Lorraine. *A Crow Doesn't Need a Shadow, A Guide to Writing Poetry From Nature*. Salt Lake City: Peregrine Books, 1994. Meant for young readers, this book provides doorways to poems inspired by the natural world.

Fox, John. *Finding What You Didn't Lose: Expressing Your Truth and Creativity Through Poem-Making*. New York: Jeremy Tarcher/Putnam, 1995. Writing poetry as a way of recapturing the joy of creativity. Chock-full of quality exercises.

————. *Poetic Medicine*. New York: Jeremy Tarcher/Putnam, 1997. This is an excellent continuation of instruction and information on writing poetry that heals.

Greenberg, David. *Teaching Poetry to Children*. Portland, OR: Continuing Education Publications. Meant for teachers of young writers, it is a simple, practical guide for new writers.

Grossman, Florence. *Getting From Here to There: Writing and Reading Poetry*. Montclair, NJ: Boynton/Cook, 1982. Full of poems by professionals and students, this anthology teaches you how to write using other's poems and strategies as springboards.

Holmes, John. *Writing Poetry*. Boston: The Writer, Inc., 1960. The author addresses the definition of a poet and includes the histories of five of his poems. He includes essays by poets Auden, Frost, Eberhart, Stevens, Williams, Moore, Wilber and Stauffer as well as a section of quotes on writing and being from poets.

Kirby, David. *Writing Poetry: Where Poems Come From and How to Write Them*. A Writer Paperback Library Book, Boston: The Writer, Inc., 1989. Reprinted 1990. This short, readable, direct book on the craft is helpful. It works with six types of strategies for poem writing and discusses publication.

Koch, Kenneth. *I Never Told Anybody: Teaching Poetry Writing in a Nursing Home*. New York: Vintage, 1977. Any of the five instructional books by master teacher and poet Kenneth Koch will be of help to you.

————. *Making Your Own Days*. New York: Simon and Schuster, 1998.

————. *Rose, Where Did You Get That Red? Teaching Great Poetry to Children*. New York: Vintage, 1972.

————. *Wishes, Lies and Dreams*. New York: Chelsea House, 1970.

———— and Kate Farrell. *Sleeping on the Wing: An Anthology of Modern Poetry With Essays on Reading and Writing*. New York: Vintage, 1982.

Kovacs, Edna. *Writing Across Cultures: A Handbook on Writing Poetry and Lyrical Prose* (From African Drum Song to Blues, Ghazal to Haiku, Villanelle to the Zoo). Hillsboro, OR: Blue Heron Publishing, Inc., 1994. Easy to follow, fun to experiment with poem writing ideas with lots of examples from new and well-published poets.

Kowit, Steve. *In the Palm of Your Hand: The Poet's Portable Workshop*. Gardiner, MN: Tilbury House, 1995. Almost as good as a live poetry writing workshop! Learn about music and metaphor, experiment and tradition in poetry as well as revision. Some help in the area of publishing, too.

Minot, Stephen. *Three Genres: The Writing of Poetry, Fiction, and Drama*, 2nd Edition. Englewood Cliffs, NJ: Prentice-Hall, 1971. The section on writing poetry includes "Six Critical Questions" to ask when revising. Also, famous poems for study.

Oliver, Mary. *A Poetry Handbook*. New York: Harcourt Brace, 1994. Serious advice that helps the poet connect the mind and heart. From a winner of the Pulitzer Prize and the National Book Award.

Packard, William. *The Poet's Dictionary: A Handbook of Prosody and Poetic Devices*. New York: Harper and Row, 1989. The author of six volumes of poems is also founder of *The New York Quarterly* and a professor of poetry at New York University. A wonderful intro by poet Karl Shapiro. The author takes over with definitions that "explore the full implications of the words 'contemporary' and 'poetry' in light of our experience in the world today."

————. *The Art of Poetry Writing: A Guide for Poets, Students, and Readers.* New York: St. Martin's Press, 1992. About poetry, its history, devices, genres, forms, nuts and bolts—all presented with thirty exercises Karl Shapiro has called "extraordinary."

Ryan, Margaret. *How to Read and Write Poems.* New York: Franklin Watts, 1991. Intended for young readers, this book by a poet in the Poets-in-Public Service program of New York City is direct, integrated and enormously useful for any beginning poet who wants references to poets, an idea of how to publish and a working experience of what a poem is.

Wallace, Robert and Michelle Boisseau. *Writing Poems.* Reading, MA: Addison Wesley Educational Publishers, 1996. May be useful if you need more ideas.

Wooldridge, Susan G. *Poemcrazy: Feeling Your Life With Words.* New York: Clarkson Potter, 1996. Exhilarating help in setting up circumstances in which poems happen.

APPENDIX II

POETS ON POETRY

(See the discussion about the Poets on Poetry series from the University of Michigan press in chapter ten):

Addonizio, Kim and Dorianne Laux. *The Poet's Companion: A Guide to the Pleasures of Writing Poetry.*

Allen, Don Cameron. *The Moment of Poetry.* Baltimore, MD: John Hopkins Press, 1962. John Holmes, May Sarton, Richard Eberhart, Richard Wilbur and Randall Jarrell write on poetry.

Anderson, Elliott and Mary Kinzie. *The Little Magazine in America: A Modern Documentary History.* Yonkers, NY: Pushcart Press, 1978. This 750-page book was produced by the combined effort of *Triquarterly* and *Pushcart.* It contains essays, memoirs, annotations and photo-materials that explore the preceding three decades of small literary magazine publishing in America.

Auden, W. H. *Making, Knowing, and Judging: An Inaugural Lecture Delivered Before the University of Oxford on 11 June 1956.* Oxford at the Calrendon Press, Oxford University Press, Amen House, London E.C.4, 1957. The master himself speaking of the way poets learn, why they write and how they write.

Bender, Sheila, ed. *The Writer's Journal: 40 Contemporary Writers and Their Journals.* New York: Dell, 1997. Poets talk about how their journal writing feeds their poetry or is their poetry.

Bender, Sheila and Christi Killien. *Writing in a New Convertible With the Top Down.* Hillsboro, OR: Blue Heron Press, 1997. Discussion and writing ideas in the form of letters and exercises.

Berg, Stephen, ed. *In Praise of What Persists.* New York: Harper & Row. Twenty-four writers sent the editor essays exploring what and who they thought were influences on their writing. Among the fiction writers, essayists and poets included are poets Richard Hugo, Tess Gallagher, Gerald Stern, Carolyn Forche, Hayden Carruth, Raymond Carver, Dave Smith and C.K. Williams.

Brown, Kurt. *The True Subject: Writers on Life and Craft.* St. Paul, MN: Graywolf Press, 1993. Best writers conference lectures including some by Gary Snyder and William Kittredge.

Chi, Lu. *Wen Fu: The Art of Writing.* Translated by Sam Hamill. Minneapolis: Milkweed Editions, 1991. Composed around 200 A.D. and gracefully translated by Mr. Hamill, this book is a joyous reference for any who read and write proetry and want to discover its pleasures and problems.

Ciardi, John. *Dialogue With an Audience.* Philadelphia and New York: J.P. Lippincott Co., 1963. In an imagined dialogue with a nonpoet, Ciardi masterfully discusses the environment of poetry, how to read poetry, and what a poet is doing when he or she is writing a poem.

———. *How a Poem Means.* Boston: Houghton Mifflin, 1959. A classic on reading poems.

———, ed. *Mid-Century American Poets.* Boston: Twayne Publishers, 1950. This collection by poets beginning to distinguish themselves by 1950 contains work by Robert Lowell, Theodore Roethke, Muriel Rukeyser, Elizabeth Bishop, Richard Wilber, Randall Jarrell, John Ciardi, Delmore Schwartz, Karl Shapiro and Richard Eberhart among others. Includes poets' own analyses of what they are doing with the craft and Ciardi's introduction about reading poetry and modern poetry.

Dobyns, Stephen. *Best Words, Best Order.* New York: St. Martin's Press, 1996. Begun by the author as craft lectures on metaphor, free verse and more for MFA students.

Dunn, Stephen. *Walking Light: Essays and Memoirs.* New York: W.W. Norton, 1993. Five of the essays are deep yet accessible discussions by a fine contemporary poet on poetry and why we write it.

Eberhart, Richard. *Of Poetry and Poets.* Urbana, IL: University of Illinois Press, 1979. Essays on poetry as a creative act and why and how a poet writes.

Eliot, T.S. *On Poetry and Poets*. New York: Farrar, Straus and Cudahy, 1957. Another master speaks on specific poets such as Yeats and Byron, and on poetry, its social function, music and voices.

Emblem, D.L. and L.D. Engdahl. *Prose Works by Poets on Poetry, a Bibliography*. The Clamshell Press, Santa Rosa, CA: 1984. Small press work and out of print, but if you can find it, it is valuable!

Foster, Jeanne. A *Music of Grace: The Sacred in Contemporary American Poetry* (American University Studies, Vol. 55). Peter Lang, New York: 1995. The author discusses the poetry of Galway Kinnell, James Wright and Anne Sexton.

Gibbons, Reginald. *The Poet's Work: 29 Masters of 20th-Century Poetry on the Origins and Practice of Their Art*. Boston: Houghton Mifflin, 1979. George Seferis, Czeslaw Milosz, Louise Bogan and W.H. Auden are among others writing here.

Glück, Louise. *Proofs & Theories: Essays on Poetry*. Hopewell, NJ: The Ecco Press, 1994. A fine collection of personal essays, reviews and literary criticism. According to *Poetry Flash* in San Francisco, it is "a prickly poetic testament and memoir of one of America's finest poets."

Hall, Donald. *Poetry: The Unsayable Said, An Essay*. Port Townsend, WA: Copper Canyon Press, 1993. A small letter press edition to celebrate the press' anniversary.

Hamburger, Michael. *The Truth of Poetry*. New York: Harcourt Brace, 1969. Effective, stirring information.

Hamill, Sam. *A Poet's Work: The Other Side of Poetry*. Seattle, WA: Broken Moon Press, 1990. An effective collection of essays that includes the wisdom of the greats.

Hass, Robert. *Twentieth-Century Pleasures, Prose on Poetry*. New York: The Ecco Press, 1984. An exceptional chapter on images from the recent poet laureate of the United States.

Heffron, Jack, ed. *The Best Writing on Writing.* Cincinnati, OH: Story Press, 1994. Advice by poets William Kittredge, Donald Hall, Kim Stafford and Adrienne Rich are included.

Hirshfield, Jane. *Nine Gates: Entering the Mind of Poetry.* New York: HarperCollins, 1997. In these essays, the poet invites readers to think about concentration, prosody, translation, originality, poetry's roots as an oral form, and the importance of the Jungian concept of shadow to art and spiritual life.

Hope, A.D. *Essays on Poetry.* Chicago: University of Chicago Press, 1965. Includes essays on the sincerity of poetry and prayer.

Hugo, Richard. *The Triggering Town: Lectures and Essays on Poetry and Writing.* New York: W.W. Norton, 1979. This is a classic. In it, the late poet and creative writing teacher lends himself to the task of doing in writing what he did in the classroom—looking at poetry from the standpoint of the writer.

Janeczko, Paul B. *Poetspeak: In Their Work, About Their Work.* New York: Collier Books, 1991. Nikki Giovanni, Joyce Carol Oates, John Updike, Peter Meinke and fifty-eight other modern American poets share themselves and their work.

Kinzie, Mary. *The Cure of Poetry in an Age of Prose: Moral Essays on the Poet's Calling.* Chicago: University of Chicago Press, 1993. Amidst much negative critiquing of poets such as Anne Sexton and Theodore Roethke, Kinzie does enhance one's reading of her much-loved Elizabeth Bishop.

Kunitz, Stanley. *A Kind of Order, A Kind of Folly: Essays and Conversations.* Boston: Little Brown and Co., 1975. Kunitz's wisdom about poetry and writing are intwined with his travels to Russia, his background in philosophy and art, and his appreciation and reviews of the poems of Theodore Roethke, Louise Bogan, Wallace Stevens, Robert Hass (as a young poet) and others of his time.

Lehman, David, ed. *Ecstatic Occasions, Expedient Forms: 85 Leading Contemporary Poets Select and Comment on Their Poems.* Ann Arbor, MI: University of Michigan Press, 1996. In the preface, Lehman says the contributions in the book demonstrate that the "process of creation and the process of discovery may coincide." Charles Simic, Frank Bidart, Mary Jo Slater, Rita Dove, Joyce Carol Oates and Richard Howard are among the eighty-five poets.

Leibowitz, Herbert, ed. *Parnassus: Twenty Years of Poetry in Review*. Ann Arbor, MI: University of Michigan Press, 1994. Parnassus was a small press literary magazine started in 1973 with the mission of treating new books of poetry as part of a new ensemble of harmonious voices. The reviews offer a good understanding of contemporary poetry.

Limmer, Ruth, ed. *Journey Around My Room: The Autobiography of Louise Bogan*. New York: Penguin, 1980. Charming writing arranged by the editor but written by the poet.

MacLeish, Archibald. *Poetry and Experience*. Boston: Houghton Mifflin, 1961. Stirring reading if you are a poet!

Mills, Ralph J. *Cry of the Human: Essays on Contemporary American Poets*. Urbana, IL: University of Illinois Press, 1975. This is a warm discussion of the personal element in American Poetry.

Nemerov, Howard, ed. *Poets on Poetry*. New York: Basic Books, 1966. Includes a wonderful essay by Jack Gilbert on American Poetry.

Neruda, Pablo. *Memoirs*. New York: Viking Penguin, 1992. An autobiography that can't help but be a poet's words on poetry entwined with a life.

O'Connell, Nicholas, ed. *At the Field's End: Interviews With 20 Pacific Northwest Writers*. Seattle, WA: Madrona Publishers, 1987. Includes David Wagoner, Carolyn Kizer, Tess Gallagher and James Mitsui among others.

Orr, Gregory and Ellen Bryant Voigt, ed. *Poets Teaching Poets, Self and the World*. Ann Arbor, MI: University of Michigan Press, 1996. Craft lectures by well-known poets presenting to MFA students.

Pac, Robert and Jay Parini, ed. *Writers on Writing: A Bread Loaf Anthology*. Hanover, NH: Middlebury College Press, 1991. The essays here are all previously unpublished and from the writers' private literary workshops. The poets represented include Marvin Bell, Stanley Elkin, Donald Justice, Erica Jong, Philip Levine, William Matthews, Linda Pastan and Ellen Bryant Voigt.

Packard, William, ed. *The Craft of Poetry: Interviews From the New York Quarterly*. New York: Doubleday, 1974. W.H. Auden, Anne Sexton, Diane Wakowski, Allen Ginsberg and Denise Levertov are among seventeen poets interviewed.

Phillips, Robert. *The Confessional Poets*. Urbana, IL: Southern Illinois University Press, 1973. Includes a good discussion of what the confessional mode in American poetry is.

Raysor, Thomas M., ed. *Wordsworth & Coleridge Selected Critical Essays*. New York: Appleton-Century-Crofts, 1958. Famous words by famous fathers of post-classical poetry in the English language.

Rilke, Rainer Maria. *Letters to a Young Poet*. Translated by M.D. Herter. New York: W.W. Norton, 1962. Famous advice from a sensitive, thoughtful poet.

Roethke, Theodore. *Straw for the Fire: From the Notebooks of Theodore Roethke 1943-63*, selected and arranged by David Wagoner. New York: Doubleday, 1974). Opportunity to see what a great poet put in his notebook pre-poem.

Rukeyser, Muriel. *The Life of Poetry*. Ashfield, MA: Paris Press, 1996. This is a much-anticipated reprinting of poet and social activist Rukeyser's 1949 treatise on poetry and its place in a democracy. "The work that a poem does," Rukeyser believes, "is a transfer of human energy."

Smith, Dave. *Local Assays: On Contemporary American Poetry*. Urbana, IL: University of Illinois Press, 1985. There are three sections in this book. In the first, the author explores his answers to the questions: What is a poem? How does a poem work? What are its limits and possibilities and why should a person spend a life making poems? The second includes discussions of the poetry of James Wright, Richard Hugo, Sylvia Plath, Robert Penn Warren, May Swenson, Louis Simpson and James Dickey. The third section is about teaching creative writing.

Strickland, Bill, ed. *On Being a Writer*. Cincinnati, OH: Writer's Digest Books, 1989. Interviews culled from the pages of three decades of *Writer's Digest Magazine*. Poets interviewed include Erica Jong, Allen Ginsberg and Nikki Giovanni.

Turner, Alberta T., ed. *50 Contemporary Poets, The Creative Process*. New York: David McKay Co., 1977. Each poet shares a poem with commentary and revision. They answer the editor's questions: How does a poem change? By what principles of technique does a poem change? How would the poets help a novice read their poems? How do the poets compare the poem with their earlier poetry?

————. *Poets Teaching: The Creative Process*. White Plains, NY: Longman Press, 1980. In eleven groups of one to three poems each by student writers, two to three distinguished poet-teachers respond to the work as they would in a workshop. Absolutely excellent reading for the study of how to think about revision and what makes a poem!

Valéry, Paul. *The Collected Works of Paul Valéry*, Vols. 1 and 2. Princeton, NJ: Bollingen Foundation, 1956, 1969. Many poets enjoy reading this master about the art of poetry.

Van Doren, Mark. *Introduction to Poetry: Commentaries on Thirty Poems*. New York: Hill and Wang, 1951. The poet chose thirty short poems he loved to read and wrote about what the poems are accomplishing and how.

Vendler, Helen. *The Given and the Made: Strategies of Poetic Redefinition*. Cambridge, MA: Harvard University Press, 1995. Discussions of the poetry of Jori Graham, Rita Dove, Robert Lowell and John Berryman. The introduction is a grand articulation of the source of poetry in a person's emotional environment.

————. *The Music of What Happens: Poems, Poets, Critics*. Cambridge, MA: Harvard University Press, 1988. The author, who has been called the best poetry critic in America today, shows what poetry does using the poems of Lionel Trilling, John Keats, Walt Whitman, Seamus Heaney, Sylvia Plath and Adrienne Rich among many others.

————. *Part of Nature, Part of Us: Modern American Poets*. Cambridge, MA: Harvard University Press, 1980. The author reads from T.S. Eliot, W.H. Auden, Wallace Stevens, Marianne Moore, Dave Smith, Robert Lowell, James Merrill, Elizabeth Bishop, Frank O'Hara, Allen Ginsberg, Frank Bidart, Louise Glück and Charles Wright among others and makes their significance clear.

————. *Soul Says: On Recent Poetry*. Cambridge, MA: The Belknap Press of Harvard University Press, 1995. Sensitive and informative readings of many fine poets, among them Seamus Heaney, Henri Cole, Amy Clampitt, Rita Dove, Jori Graham, Allen Ginsberg, Charles Simic and Gary Snyder.

Whyte, David. *The Heart Aroused: Poetry and Preservation of the Soul in Corporate America*. New York: Doubleday, 1994. In the author's words, the poet needs the practicalities of making a living to test and temper the lyricism of insight and observations. The corporation needs the poet's insight and powers of attention in order to weave the inner world of soul and creativity with the outer world of form and matter.

Williams, William Carlos. *I Wanted to Write a Poem: The Autobiography of the Works of a Poet*. Boston: Beacon Press, 1958. The great poet writes about ideas and impulses behind his poems as well as the magazines and poets he was in touch with over the years.

BOOKS ON ART AND CREATIVITY

Bennett, Hal Zina. *Write From the Heart, Unleashing the Power of Your Creativity*. Mill Valley, CA: Nataraj, 1995. Convincing personal experience essays.

Berendt, Joachim-Ernst. *The Third Ear: On Listening to the World*. New York: Holt, 1985. In this provocative book, the author suggests that compassion, receptivity, peacefulness and spirituality are connected to the ear and that the way to wisdom is through the ear.

Cameron, Julia. *The Artist's Way*. New York: Putnam, 1995. Many writers have been encouraged in their process by studying, practicing and even taking workshops in these ideas.

Cousineau, Phil. *Soul: An Archaeology: Readings from Socrates to Ray Charles*. San Francisco: Harper San Francisco, 1994.

Gardner, Howard. *Creating Minds*. New York: Basic Books, 1996. Among the great minds he investigates to analyze creativity is the poet T.S. Eliot's.

———. *Frames of Mind: The Theory of Multiple Intelligences*. New York: Basic Books, 1985. One of the intelligences discussed is the linguistic with which poets are endowed.

Hillman, James. *The Soul's Code: In Search of Character and Calling*. New York: Warner, 1997. An interesting discussion of how we find out what we are on earth for and what is our calling.

Koestler, Arthur. *The Act of Creation*. New York: Dell Publishing, 1964. Words from the famed author of *Darkness at Noon* and over thirty other novels.

May, Rollo. *The Courage to Create*. New York: Bantam, 1978. An extended essay on what creativity requires, how it happens and why it is ultimately unsuppressible.

———. *The Cry of Myth*. New York: W.W. Norton, 1991.

Metzger, Deena. *Writing for Your Life*. San Francisco: Harper San Francisco, 1992. Anecdotes and exercises to keep your sensibilities fresh.

Moore, Thomas. *The Care of the Soul*. New York: Harper Collins, 1992. What is poetry but careful care of the soul?

O'Hara, Nancy. *Just Listen: A Guide to Finding Your Own True Voice*. New York: Bantam Doubleday Dell, 1997. The author is a Buddhist who has studied practices for finding one's self in a busy world.

Phillips, Jan. *Marry Your Muse: Making a Lasting Commitment to Your Creativity*. Wheaton, IL: Quest Books, 1997. This book teaches the artist's creed and how to affirm it in oneself through thoughtful, joyous practice.

Rico, Gabriel Luccor. *Writing the Natural Way: Using Right Brain Techniques to Release Your Expressive Powers*. Los Angeles: J.P. Tarcher, 1983. A strong guide to the use of clustering for inviting the unconsious and its handle on details into the writing process.

APPENDIX IV

POETRY ANTHOLOGIES

Allen, Donald M., ed. *The New American Poetry*. New York: Grove Press, 1960. Forty-four poets identified in 1960 as part of America's vital modern poetry movement: the late Allen Ginsberg, Charles Olson, Robert Duncan and Denise Levertov among them.

Anglesey, Zoe. *Stone on Stone Poetry by Women of Diverse Heritages*, Seattle, WA: Open Hand Publishing, 1994. Sharon Doubiago, C.D. Wright and Carolyn Forche and among many others. In Spanish and English.

Basho. *Monkey's Raincoat: Linked Poetry of the Basho School With Haiku Selections*. Translated by Lenore Mayhew. Boston: Charles E. Tuttle Co, 1985. A good selection and fine to emulate!

Bender, Sheila and Phil Tobin, ed. *The Poem and the World: An International Anthology*. Seattle, WA: Poem and the World, Richard Hugo House, Books i, ii, iii, iv, and v from 1993 to 1998.

Brant, Beth, ed. *A Gathering of Spirit: A Collection of North American Indian Woman*. Ithaca, NY: Firebrand Books, 1988. Poems by Linda Hogan, Joy Harjo and Elizabeth Woody among many others.

Broughton, Irv, ed. *A Good Man: Fathers and Sons in Poetry and Prose*. New York: Fawcett, Columbine, 1993. e.e. cummings, Charles Wright and Richard Blessing among other poets sprinkled amidst the prose pieces.

Canan, Janine, ed. *She Rises Like the Sun, Invocations of the Goddess by Contemporary American Women Poets*. Freedom, CA: The Crossing Press, 1989. Jana Harris, Maya Angelou, May Sarton, Audre Lorde and Marge Piercy are among the women who sing the praises of the Goddess.

Chester, Laura and Sharon Barba, eds. *Rising Tides: 20th-Century American Women Poets*. New York: Washington Square Press, 1973. Introduction by Anaïs Nin. Seventy women poets included Adrienne Rich, Nikki Giovanni and Lyn Lifshin.

Conanoe, Joel, ed. *Eight American Poets, An Anthology*. New York: Random House, 1994. Roethke, Bishop, Lowell, Berryman, Sexton, Plath, Ginsberg and Merrill are represented. Biographies preceed the excellent selection of each poet's work.

Cosman, Carol, Joan Keefe, and Kathleen Weaver, eds. *The Penguin Book of Women Poets*. New York: Penguin Books Ltd., 1978. Poetry by women from around the world, 1567 B.C. to contemporary times.

Dacey, Philip and David Jauss. *Strong Measures: Contemporary American Poetry in Traditional Forms*. New York: Harper and Row, 1986. Donald Hall, Stephen Dunn, Marilyn Hacker and many others writing in form.

Ferlinghetti, Lawrence. *City Lights Pocket Poets Anthology*. San Francisco: City Lights, 1996. Celebrates forty years of publishing and cultural history by being a retrospective on the influential City Lights Pocket Poets Series.

Finch, Annie. *A Formal Feeling Comes: Poems in Form by Contemporary Women*. Brownsville, OR: Story Line Press, 1994. The editor chose examples from sixty contemporary American women poets who have transformed and strengthened their literary inheritance. The poets represented have written comments on form and how they view and work with it.

Forche, Carolyn. *Against Forgetting: Twentieth-Century Poetry of Witness*. New York: W.W. Norton, 1993. Poems from many centuries and parts of the world that document the sufferings and struggles of the twentieth century and the ability of poets and poetry to persevere.

Hampl, Patricia. *Burning Bright: An Anthology of Sacred Poetry*. New York: Ballantine Books, 1995. From the great monotheistic religions of the West, the editor gathered over a hundred poems of faith, spiritual longing and devout belief. She has ordered them by time of day—Morning, Noon and Night—as western prayer cycles are ordered. Included are Yeats, Hopkins, Milosz, Plath, Rilke, Stevens, Tsvetaeva and Clifton among others.

Hamill, Sam. *The Erotic Spirit: An Anthology of Poems of Sensuality, Love and Longing*. Boston: Shambhala, 1996. Poetry from the fifteenth century B.C. to the present; biblical, Shakespearian and feminist.

Heyen, William. *The Generation of 2000: Contemporary American Poets*. Princeton, NJ: Ontario Review Press, 1984. The editor, a fine poet himself, collected the work of thirty poets plus himself to explore the generation of poets born between 1934 and 1949 who were coming to poetic maturity in the 1980s. Ai, Gallagher, Hass, Strand, Plumly, McHugh, Clifton, Goldbarth, Carver, Glück and Matthews are among those whose work is included. Each poet has opening remarks about poetry and how they write it, and the selections include their earlier work as well as poems of the 1980s.

Howe, Florence. *No More Masks: An Anthology of Twentieth-Century American Women Poets*. New York: Harper Perennial, 1993.) The work of one hundred women poets.

Knight, Brenda and Anne Waldman, eds. *Women of the Beat Generation: The Writers, Artists, and Muses at the Heart of a Revolution*. Berkeley, CA: Conari Press, 1996. The collection profiles forty women writers and artists, showcases their work, and reveals the Beat movement through the eyes of women who were there.

Lehman, David, senior ed. *The Best American Poetry of 1996*. New York: Simon & Schuster, 1996. Adrienne Rich did the intro and chose the issue's poems. In its ninth year in 1996, each year's volume remains one of the best anthologies available. It has long biographies of the contributing poets and lists the magazines where the poems were found. *Manoa, River Styx, TriQuarterly, Colorado Review*, and *Many Mountains Moving* were among the magazines represented in 1996.

Merrill, Christopher. *Forgotten Language, Contemporary Poets and Nature*. Salt Lake City, UT: Peregrine Smith Books, 1991. The poems are by the best and each is a "plea on behalf of the wild—in the natural world and in poetry itself."

Moyer, Bill. *The United States of Poetry*. New York: Harry N. Abrams, 1996. This is a beautiful book of poets and poems from around the country.

Murphy, George Jr. *The Poet's Choice*. Green Harbor, MA: Tendril Magazine, 1980. One hundred poets submitted their favorite from their body of work. Ai, Robert Bly, Robert Hass, Raymond Carver, Maxine Kumin, Sharon Olds and Diane Wakoski among others.

Perrine, Laurence. *Sound and Sense: An Introduction to Poetry*. New York: Harcourt Brace, 1977. Using poems by Tennyson, Shakespeare, Hardy, Plath, MacLeish, the Brownings, Yeats, Herbert, Donne, e.e. cummings, Milton and Joyce among others, the author addresses a discussion of the elements of poetry including imagery, figurative language, allusion, tone, rhythm and meter.

Sato, Hiroaki and Burton Watson, eds. *From the Country of Eight Islands: An Anthology of Japanese Poetry*. Seattle, WA: University of Washington Press, 1981. A great collection for studying lyrical qualities in poetry. These poems are from ancient to modern times.

Sewell, Marilyn, ed. *Claiming the Spirit Within: A Sourcebook of Women's Poetry*. Boston: Beacon Press, 1996. Poems by American women organized by theme: from this we come, by this we live, from fullness we give, we bless those who follow. Includes work by Sandra Cisneros, Lucille Clifton, Rita Dove, Joy Harjo, Denise Levertov and Kathleen Norris.

Simpson, Louis. *An Introduction to Poetry*. New York: St. Martin's Press, 1986. A classic anthology with an introduction by the poet discussing meter, rhyme, stanza and sound. The poetry included in his large volume includes that of Chaucer, Marvell, Blake, Wordsworth, Coleridge, Whitman, Hardy, Hopkins, Dickinson, Eliot, Stevens, Frost, Pound, Millay, Jeffers, Nash, Auden, Thomas, Wilber, Dickey, Levertov, Kizer, Bly, O'Hara, Creely, Ginsberg, Sexton, Wright and Heaney among many more.

Stallworthy, Jon, ed. *A Book of Love Poetry*. New York: Oxford University Press, 1973. More than 190 poets; funny, sad, tender and erotic.

Strand, Mark, ed. *The Contemporary American Poets, American Poetry Since 1940*. New York: New American Library, 1969. Louise Glück, Caroline Kizer, James Dickey and eighty-nine others who sparked a renaissance of poetry.

Vendler, Helen. *The Harvard Book of Contemporary American Poetry*. Cambridge, MA: The Belknap Press of Harvard University Press, 1985. Thirty-five poets were selected by the author who presents their work progressing from earlier to later poems. Brief biographies of each poet are appended. Among the outstanding poets are Adrienne Rich, Mark Strand, Robert Pinsky, John Berryman, Anne Sexton and Michael Blumenthal.

INDIVIDUAL POET'S COLLECTIONS TO LOOK FOR

The best way to find poetry collections you might want to read is by finding current reviews of poetry books, looking on the shelves of stores with good poetry collections, and going to libraries, poetry centers and writer's workshops where faculty poets bring their books and suggest other poets to read. You can also check for poets in the year's Best Poetry collection and see what collections they have in print.

Here is a list of poets currently on my shelves, in small and large press publications.

Ai
Sherman Alexie
Agha Shahid Ali
Jody Aliason
Philip Appleman
Christine Balk
Judith Barrington
Bruce Beasley
Marvin Bell
Beth Bentley
Nelson Bentley
Wendell Berry
James Bertolino
Frank Bidart
Linda Bierds
Elizabeth Bishop
William Blake
Richard Blessing
Joseph Brodsky
James Broughton
Sharon Bryan
Raymond Carver
Thomas Centolella
Henri Cole
Sandra Cisneros
Lucille Clifton
Madeline DeFrees
James Dickey
Emily Dickinson

Chitra Divakaruni
Rita Dove
Stephen Dunn
Cornellius Eady
Carolyn Forche
Robert Francis
Kathleen Fraser
Robert Frost
Tess Gallagher
Paula Jones Gardiner
Reginald Gibbons
Jack Gilbert
Allen Ginsberg
Louise Glück
Patricia Goedicke
Jori Graham
Linda Gregg
Sam Hamill
Joy Harjo
Robert Hass
Samuel Hazo
Seamus Heaney
Brenda Hillman
Jane Hirschfield
Linda Hogan
Alicia Hokanson
Garrett Hongo
Judith Hougan
Ted Hughes

Richard Hugo

Fled Brown Jackson

Sybil James

Laura Jensen

Shirley Kaufman

Jane Kenyon

Galway Kinnell

Carolyn Kizer

Maxine Kumin

Stanley Kunitz

Dorianne Laux

David Lee

Li-Young Lee

Denise Levertov

Philip Levine

Larry Levis

Audre Lorde

Sandra MacPherson

Donna Masini

William Matthews

Heather McCue

Colleen McElroy

Peter Meinke

James Merrill

W.S. Merwin

James Mitsui

Kyoko Mori

Carol Muske

Pablo Neruda

Duane Niatum

Naomi Shihab Nye

Frank O'Hara

Diana O'Herir

Sharon Olds

Mary Oliver

Gregory Orr

Linda Pastan

Marge Piercy

Robert Pinsky

Sylvia Plath

Stanley Plumly

Lawrence Raab

Alberto Rhea

Adrienne Rich

David Rigsbee

Rainer Marie Rilke

Theodore Roethke

Patti Anne Rogers

Vern Rutsala

Sandra Sanchez

Sappho

May Sarton

Anne Sexton

Charles Simic

Judith Skillman

Gary Snyder

Gary Soto

William Stafford

Wallace Stevens

Mark Strand

Joyce Sutphen

Dylan Thomas

Quincy Troupe

Mona Van Duyn

Sharon Van Sluys

Reetika Vazirani

David Wagoner

Emily Warn

Walt Whitman

C.K. Williams

William Carlos Williams

Shawn Wong

Elizabeth Woody

William Wordsworth

James Wright

Al Young

INDEX